Classroom Management

Bright Ideas
for Early Years

Published by Scholastic Ltd
Villiers House, Clarendon Avenue,
Leamington Spa, Warwickshire
CV32 5PR

© 1994 Scholastic Ltd
34567890 67890

Edited by Elizabeth Miles
Illustrations by Jane Andrews
Photographs by Anne Crabbe (page 5),
Keith Hawkins (page 9), Chris Kelly (page
19), Bob Bray (pages 27 and 47), Pete
Corbett (page 37), Richard Butchins (page
55), L.L. Fahidy (page 65)
Cover design by Micky Pledge
Cover photograph by Fiona Pragoff
Artwork by David Harban Design,
Warwick
Typeset by Typesetters (Birmingham) Ltd
Printed in Great Britain by the Alden
Press Ltd, Oxford

British Library Cataloguing in Publication Data
A catalogue record for this book is available from the British
Library

ISBN 0-590-53072-0

Contents

Introduction

Teaching young children is a very demanding job. The skills of the early years educator are many, but high on the list of priorities have to be the skills of classroom management and organisation (Jones and Jones, 1986). Without a well-ordered environment and a system for operating it, the teacher–child relationship, so vital to early years education, will not have the opportunity to develop effectively. A sound underlying organisation and management of the learning environment for three- to six-year-olds is crucial to educators' and children's feelings of success, achievement and well-being, and for promoting opportunities for supported learning and individual development. Entering a pleasing and well-run environment also gives parents and carers confidence that they are placing their precious 'charges' into the hands of caring and competent people.

A shared responsibility

The class space has to be flexible, dynamic and interesting, with each designated area capable of accommodating a wide variety of activities, while retaining commitment to a sense of order from everyone concerned.

Children must feel that it is as much their environment as the adults', and so need to share vital information such as how and why the class base is organised as it is. (The term 'class base' is used here to include any type of class area.)

Given that children have lapses of memory like the rest of us, it is nevertheless surprising when they appear not to know the location of basic materials such as crayons, scissors or LEGO. This reflects the notion of education as something someone else imposes upon them rather than the idea of children being in on the 'secrets' — and the process — from the beginning (Edwards and Mercer, 1987). The class base is the domain of both adults and children and each must share both the knowledge and responsibility for its structure and contents (Moyles, 1992).

Viewpoints and principles

What is it that underlies classroom organisation, routines, rules, structures and daily events? What should early years educators consider when contemplating the issues of good classroom management? No doubt each of us, starting as we do from different viewpoints, will offer differing emphases. However, there are certain organisational and management principles which most people will readily agree upon. Jones and Jones (1986) suggest three basic skills which teachers should possess:
- planning and getting things ready;
- knowledge of the age phase and what is to be taught;
- understanding of children and learning.

All of these are relative of course and, although ostensibly simple, hide a multitude of beliefs and knowledge needed to underpin their full development in the classroom.

Educators need to be aware of their own beliefs and assumptions when it comes to organising and managing the

class base, and it may be necessary to begin by challenging the integrity of these. For example, what are your priorities in developing the class base? Is your overriding rationale essentially pedagogic (making the most of teaching and learning opportunities) or social (ensuring constant opportunities for sharing and caring between those involved)? The curriculum may appear to be the overriding demand for some people. For others, the views of parents may take precedence. Clearly, all these must be considered but, above all, the class base must serve the needs of the children. Their needs include opportunities to:
• be independent;
• make choices;
• gain knowledge and understanding;
• develop skills;
• learn from adults and each other;
• care and be cared for;
• share and be tolerant;
• make — and break — rules;
• be messy, as well as clean and tidy;
• construct — and destroy;
• listen, talk and communicate;
• make marks (preferably legitimately!);
• be noisy — and quiet at times;
• be alone and together;
• be physically active;
• be adventurous and curious;
• be relaxed and comfortable;
• be artists and designers;
• be observers and ask questions;
• be manipulators (of things and people!);
• be imaginative and creative;
• succeed;
• be themselves!

About this book

How far does your class base facilitate all the above? Could it do so more effectively? Through the activities in this book attention will be drawn to a range of issues related to dealing with the youngest children in educational settings. In relation specifically to a pleasant, well-organised and well-displayed environment we look at general routines and structure; easily accessible materials; the beginnings and endings of sessions; the planning and monitoring of activities; the needs of other adults such as parents and carers in understanding the system; the provision for play-based activities; and the use of time.

The problem with a play-based curriculum is that it is inevitably messy, rendering it even more important that there is a place for everything and everything is in its place! Many early years bases are large and, quite rightly, organised into smaller bays or areas (Field, 1980) with either a topic or curriculum focus, such as the Investigation Area, the Story Corner or the Three Bears Cottage, thus giving an appropriate 'homely' feel for the children and a sense of both scale and security. If these areas are also utilised for the storage of relevant materials in ways which give children and adults ready access, a number of organisational needs are satisfied.

While this book offers practical ideas towards sound organisation and management, the emphasis must be on educators to stand back and reflect objectively on their own settings, remembering the range of activities in which both adults and children are involved. An overriding principle must be 'Stand back, look hard, watch and wonder why'! Then talk to both the adults *and* the children.

Place and space

Chapter one

Do you ever wish you had more space, more storage facilities, better distributed floor space, a square area instead of a rectangle, a raised floor, not a sunken floor, more windows, fewer doors or better located electric sockets? Well, whatever the area or siting of the class base you find yourself in, it is futile to wish it were different! A better use of time and energy is to concentrate on the good points of your new or existing base.

It will require some careful thought and time to ensure you are working with the full potential of the base and perhaps overcoming its limitations. But the rewards of careful planning may well be reaped several times over when the class base is operating efficiently and smoothly.

Even if you feel you 'know' the space well, it is still vital to make a basic plan of the available area and gather information regarding furniture, resources and materials. It is surprising how many unused resources, never mind unused or poorly used spaces, one finds during a basic review of this kind.

Reviewing the potential of the base in relation to previous practice is also vital in existing bases. It is all too easy to ignore a frayed carpet or climb repeatedly over a badly located piece of equipment when a brief review of the situation could have prompted immediate action. As for those human traffic jams at certain times in the day or the perpetually demolished display – can these be overcome? The shape and space (even the name) given to an area within the class base have all been shown to affect the way children operate in the classroom (Nash, 1981; Craig, 1991) and in many classrooms the carpet area – although vital at certain times in the day – is frequently underused at others.

Most adults dealing with young children will tend to think of the class base as a substitute 'home'. Curtains, interesting dividers, colour co-ordination, carpeting, separated 'rooms' and attention to how the place looks will add to its homely feel, as may plants and small animals. However, because children come from different types of homes, the class base has to be an amalgam of different cultures and ethnic backgrounds.

It should also be remembered that children with special needs, such as a disabled or partially sighted child, will want to find evidence of their lives in the classroom surroundings. Ensuring that the doorway to the home corner is made sufficiently wide for wheelchairs and that there is space to get a wheelchair to the table are also vital features.

Making a ground plan

Objective
To achieve a clear picture of all available space in and around the class base and consider the most efficient and effective location of furniture and resources.

What you need
Large squared paper with at least 5cm-squares.

What to do
Either measure the classroom area and translate each square metre (or half metre) onto one square of the paper or pace out the classroom in equal-sized strides, transferring each stride to a square. (See Figures 1 and 2 for sample

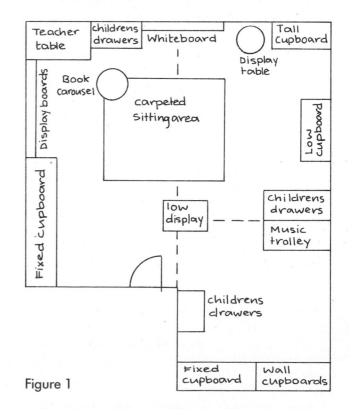

Figure 1

Adapted from *Organizing for Learning in the Primary Classroom*, J. Moyles (Open University Press)

10

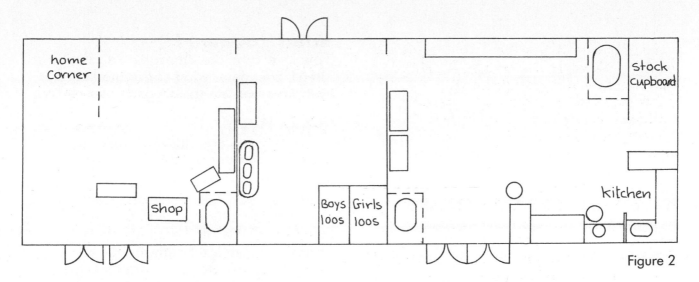

Figure 2

plans.) Remember to include all alcoves, stock cupboards and odd corners. Also measure any complementary spaces around the perimeter of the class base including, for example, usable corridor or cloakroom areas.

Draw on your plan, preferably to scale, all the fixed items such as windows, fitted cupboards and power points.

Variation

If the base is fairly clear or can be cleared of movable furniture and resources, take a series of photographs of parts of the room and mount them into a collage giving an overall view of the area. Photographs could be used in any case to support the development of the basic ground plan.

What goes where?

Objective

To decide upon the location of specific furniture, furnishings and resources in order to develop the efficient and effective storage, access and retrieval of equipment.

What you need

Plain and squared paper, pens.

What to do

Think about the main areas of interest (or curriculum foci) you want in the class base. Three basic areas or bays could be Investigation, Language and Creative areas (Moyles, 1993), good because they can all be subdivided further into, for example, noisy, quiet, messy, construction and art areas. Next consider:
● where water, power points, fixed cupboards and heavy 'traffic' areas are sited;
● where carpets, large storage, quiet and noisy areas are best located (Should a painting area be close to the carpet? Will children be able to read quietly next to the construction area?);
● whether the disabled child will be able to gain equal access to all the activities.

Draw on your plan where you feel each area and its resources would be best located.

Variation

Use cut-out scale drawings of all items of movable furniture (it is not necessary to include small chairs) and storage. Place the drawings on the plan and shuffle them around until you get a good feel for the occupied space.

Positioning furniture

Objective
To consider the use of the edges and middles of a class base.

What you need
A willingness to think about and try another way!

What to do
In many class bases, storage is all around the edge of the room and children are mostly in the middle, where they constantly have to pass by each other. Look at your base. Could some of the peripheral furniture be brought into the middle to create storage areas? Could some of the children's furniture or cosy areas be moved to the edges to create quieter areas with less human traffic.

Follow-up
Corridors and alcoves can usefully be considered, too, in the search for more small areas.

Creating cosy spaces

Objective
To create smaller areas within a large base so that children can feel more 'at home' and have a greater opportunity for concentration and small group activities.

What you need
Low-level furniture, storage or display areas, one metre wide corrugated card, storage crates on castors.

What to do
Having decided on the main areas or bays within the class base (see 'What goes where?', page 11), locate furniture in the desired position, placing storage cupboards, crates and display stands at angles to divide off the designated spaces. If these are insufficient or unavailable, sandwich corrugated card between two or more work tables to divide off the areas. The card can also be made to curve round corners.

Move around and check that you can see over the divisions from all angles in the base. Move around at child height and make sure it feels cosy rather than cage-like.

Variation
Pieces of curtain on wires can be suspended between two cupboards or display boards. Wooden or plastic trellis tacked in the space between two cupboards is also effective as it allows through-vision or hanging items to be displayed.

Walk this way!

Objective
To lessen traffic jams and diminish disturbance, usually in smaller class bases, by plotting prescribed routes around it.

What you need
Cardboard cut-outs of footprints in different sizes, double-sided sticky-tape.

What to do

Plot the most suitable pathways between the various areas of the classroom, letting the children make some of the decisions. Stick the footprints down following the safest, most well-conceived paths. Make up a game to teach the children how to use them. Do not let the adults infringe the 'rules' either!

If you have physically disabled children make the pathways wide enough to ensure their mobility, perhaps laying out tracks as well as footprints?

Variation

Footprints could be in different colours, changing as they move from bay to bay. They could also have the area or bay name written on them in whatever languages are appropriate, or in different number systems. They are easily changed if areas alter.

Adding a few touches

Objective

To brighten up and develop particular areas, such as the home corner, with a view to offering implicit curriculum opportunities for the children.

What you need

A range of fabric pieces in primary colours (striped, plain, spotted and checked), towelling, odd scraps of braid, lace or other trimmings, a sewing machine, sewing thread.

What to do

Decide what you are making from your resources:
● towelling can be made into large, medium and small towels (for large, medium and small home-corner 'occupants' like the three bears);

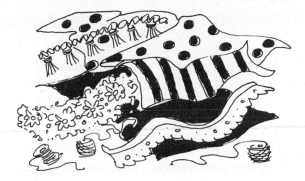

● cotton material can be made into matching and co-ordinated tablecloths and placemats or curtains and tea-towels;
● edgings can be used for fringing on the towels and lace on the tablemats.

The items need not be contained in home corners but can also be used for drinks time, picnics and displays. Having this type of resource encourages children to keep any area neat and tidy and gives both play experiences and tidy-up time a great potential for learning!

Colour it calm

Objective

To consider the best colours for different areas of the room to achieve the desired working and playing conditions.

What you need

Fabrics, paints, coloured card, clear self-adhesive plastic.

What to do

Look around in shops, banks, offices and at home to discover the colours that make you feel calm or excited, and make you want to explore. Soft greens are usually used in areas of quiet; reds are used for warmth; and blues for cool areas.

13

Think about the areas or bays in the class base and decide what you want them to convey. Use an appropriate colour to do whatever is necessary to suit the mood of the area. Large-scale jobs would be making curtains or cushions, painting the dividing screens or even the furniture. Simple but effective tasks would be covering the cupboard tops with coloured card and clear self-adhesive plastic, and appropriately coloured labelling.

Variations
● Keep all the storage boxes and trays in an area in a particular colour or use the relevant backing colour on picture displays.
● Develop a colour theme with the children and let them make decisions on colour moods.

A passport to action

Objective
To encourage children to make predetermined choices about where they work and play.

What you need
'Passports' made by putting photographs or drawings of the children on the front of folded card about 8 × 12cm in size, with areas of the classroom named (or pictorially represented) inside.

What to do
The children are given their 'passports' during group time and then, perhaps in discussion with the adult, decide which areas or bays they would like to 'visit' during the session. They can either put a tick by the area's name or picture, or circle it. If marks are made in pencil the passports can be used again. The

children then take their passports to the areas of their choice and use them for 'entry'. Adults can 'stamp' the passport entries to that area and, in so doing, will be monitoring individual children's activities and ensuring the sensible use of the space in each designated area by limiting choices or encouraging different choices.

Follow-up
Once the system is in place let the children make their own decisions.
● Blank loose pages inside the 'passport' can be used when children are adept at making their own choices and can draw in pictures of where they want to go by themselves.
● Passports for bi-lingual children should also be written in different languages.

Space for big paper

Objective
To store large paper and card for easy access by children and adults.

What you need
Large, empty, straight-sided glue or paint buckets, gloss paint or coloured paper and glue.

What to do
Make sure the buckets are empty and clean. Remove any handles, then paint or cover the buckets to hide the original labelling. Curl batches of large sheets of paper and stand them in the buckets. (A3 is best, although A2 will work if the buckets are sufficiently large.) Different buckets can be used for different colours and the covering to the bucket can indicate its contents.

Variation
The handles can be left on and the buckets suspended from hooks under shelving to save floor space.

A place for big bricks

Objective
To store very large bricks in a very small space.

What you need
Any available wall space, corner or alcove.

What to do
Instead of putting interlocking bricks such as DUPLO into a box, let the children build a shallow, flat wall with them against an existing wall. This takes up very little space and means they are readily available for use.

Follow-up
Think about brick-laying patterns and create 'accurate' walls in different 'bonds' with appropriate bricks. Collect pictures or rubbings to help the children with their brick-laying.

Small-space displays

Objective
To think about original displays for small areas, odd corners or alcoves, and create display areas where wall space is limited.

What you need
A selection of items to display (the following examples use spider and robot creations), a hoop, thread, grocery boxes, sticky-tape, glue, paint, kitchen paper, string.

What to do
• A spider display. Help the children to make a 'web' by stretching thread across the hoop, securing it with tape on the edges if necessary. Hang paper spiders or spider pictures and perhaps descriptive writing from the threads. Hang the hoop from the ceiling (two or three can hang together at different heights).
• A robot display. Make a large robot with the children from grocery boxes, covering them with kitchen paper and painting them a suitable colour with very large brushes (alternatively, boxes could be covered with coloured paper before being glued together). Stand the robot in a corner with pictures, writing and small models displayed on different parts of it.

Follow-up

Basic hanging display boards for repeated use can be made by covering very thick card (perhaps two or more layers of grocery box card) with hessian or felt and attaching a length of ribbon or strong tape. These boards have the advantage of turning gently to reveal differing images on either side.

Small display shelves

Objective

To create a three-dimensional display for small artefacts or to give pride of place to children's models.

What you need

Thick card, household paint (gloss or emulsion) or sticky-backed plastic, string, pins, scissors.

What to do

Cut the card to your preferred size for shelves. They can range from very small (10×20cm) to very large (about 30× 30cm), beyond which they get heavy and unmanageable. It is useful to have a range of shelf sizes stored away so that you have just the right one for any occasion. Divide the cut card in half lengthways and score the fold without cutting it through. Bend the card away from the score, and then paint or cover the card on both sides.

When dry, punch a hole about 1.5cm in from each corner. Cut two pieces of string and thread each piece from a base corner to a top corner, drawing them up until the card is at a 90° angle (see Figure 1). Pin the card to the wall with long drawing pins or dressmakers' pins.

Variations

● If a back to the display is not needed, small grocery boxes can be utilised by threading strings through the top at all four corners and making the back strings shorter than the front so that the top lies flat (see Figure 2).
● The card could be covered with cork or polystyrene tiles, wrapping paper, wallpaper or sandpaper (for texture and grip).

Creating display areas

Objective

To create a flexible display area for two-dimensional items where wall space is limited.

What you need

Corrugated card (1m or 1.5m wide) on a roll, long cardboard tubes (those from the centre of floor coverings or stout mapping tubes are best) or spare chairs, small furniture, stage blocks.

What to do

Roll out the card in an upright position, swirling it across the available space. If the roll is large, the loosely wound ends will, with a little teasing out, support

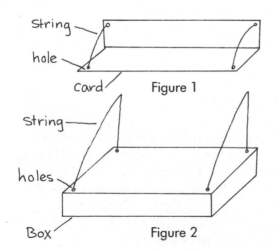

String
hole
Card   Figure 1

String
holes
Box   Figure 2

themselves, particularly with the help of a strong cardboard tube (see Figure 1). Alternatively, one end can be stapled to an available wall with the rest flowing out and wound round a piece of furniture or a stage block (see Figure 2).

The whole roll of corrugated card can be wound round two chairs (or other furniture) placed at a suitable distance apart and pinned, stapled or taped together to form a continuous loop, allowing for displays on both sides.

Variation

A display panel (for use over a window or brick wall) can be made by attaching the edge of a piece of corrugated card to a stout cardboard tube with glue or tape, looping strong string through the tube to make a hanging. The bottom of the card can be ballasted with another tube or a wooden batten.

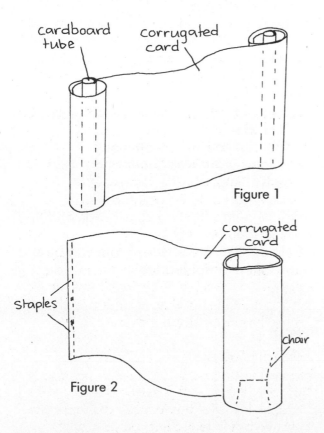

Figure 1

Figure 2

Table treasures

Objective

To provide a pleasant environment for groups of seated children.

What you need

Small pots or trays of interesting dried flowers, twigs, leaves or small artefacts, interesting pebbles — any of these can be seasonal, topic related or ethnically oriented.

What to do

Occasionally, before children arrive, set out something interesting in an attractive way on some or all of the work spaces and encourage the children to talk about the objects with parents or other available adults and peers.

Children's own displays

Objective

To encourage children to think about their role in creating and maintaining a pleasant classroom environment.

What you need

A child-height display board (with a flat surface beneath if you wish), different sized coloured papers.

What to do

Nothing! Leave it to the children. Simply encourage and help them to display pieces of their own work or models in an interesting and aesthetic way. They can learn to mount two-dimensional works with borders and place models on their own self-made display mats. Appropriate labels can be added.

17

Enabling co-operative art work

Objectives
To allow for co-operative painting or collage and to create a vertical painting area where no easels are available.

What you need
A free-standing, stable display panel, polythene sheeting, a tray of paints or collage materials, newspaper.

What to do
Cover the board on both sides with polythene sheeting. Place the paints or collage materials on newspaper on the floor. The space in which two or three children can readily stand together will encourage them to work co-operatively. Let the children select their own paper on which to paint or do the collage and allow them to plan the outcome together.

Variation
Two groups can work at the stand, one on either side, which gives so much more space than the usual easel. Very large co-operative pictures can be undertaken.

Creating a monster!

Objective
To create a double-sided and interesting bookshelf arrangement or display area.

What you need
Very large, thick cardboard longer and taller than the furniture you will be using, a felt-tipped pen, a craft knife, sticky-tape, paint or coloured paper and pens, two low cupboards or two tables.

What to do
Sandwich the cardboard between the two low cupboards or tables so that it sticks out all round and tape the two pieces of furniture together, or you could join them with a thin batten and nails. Draw a monster shape on the cardboard with head, spines, tail — do not make anything too thin and fragile as it needs to be robust — and cut the shape out. Let the children paint or decorate both sides with felt-tipped pens or coloured sticky paper. Set out the books or display on both sides.

Variations
• You can create any animal — elephants work well. Trees and shrubs are also simple and effective. The cardboard could be painted before attaching it to the two cupboards and cutting it out.
• Made with wood, the shape can be a more permanent feature.

Routines and rituals

Chapter two

There is no doubt that all young children love routine and are happiest in a predictable environment. Routines engender confidence and self-assurance, and allow young children the security necessary if they are to explore materials and situations in a socially 'safe' framework. However, routines should never become boring and the occasional change (developing a new play area or setting up displays to generate new interests) will be a good stimulus for the children and adults.

With routines come rules and the related issue of safety. The rules should be both few in number and clearly explained to the children, preferably in the context of the children's own decision-making and safety considerations. Adults also need to think about whether all the rules currently imposed are necessary.

Routines and rules also exist as behaviour controls. Excitable children can easily lose their self-esteem if they are constantly chastised for 'being naughty'. It is far better to generate on-going self-discipline by supporting appropriate behaviour (rather than by nagging the bad).

Routines and rituals give both adults and children a sense of security and purpose. This is particularly so for children — and their parents and carers — when they first join the group, and for those children needing emotional security. Access to all materials for all children can be more effectively encouraged and ensured where children's activities are monitored in a structured system.

A range of activities for working in a secure but exciting framework constitute this chapter.

Structuring the day

Objective
To review existing practices and consider potential changes to the structure of the day.

What you need
An itemised timetable of a general week in the life of your class base.

What to do
Complete your timetable for this week, then consider:
• What curriculum balances does it offer?
• What are individual children's experiences likely to be? Does this represent a balance in relation to the curriculum? Are there self-chosen and directed activities? Are there sufficient opportunities for physical activity?

• What demands does it make of the adults in the classroom? Can these really be fulfilled adequately?

Discuss the timetable as a team and make any adjustments necessary. (The planning sheets in the next activity may help.)

Follow-up
Curriculum balance is probably more effectively examined in relation to weekly, fortnightly, monthly or half-termly reviews.

Balancing the day

Objective
To think about the balance of the day for children and adults in relation to curriculum and activities.

What you need
A pen, your own usual planning sheets, photocopiable pages 83 and 84.

What to do
Hold a team meeting to plot on the sheets the planned activities for the week, making any adjustments to your provision as appropriate. Are there any gaps? Is any section overloaded?

By having this information it is possible to ensure that over each week, suitably varied provision is made for both activities and curriculum coverage. Adjust the plan as necessary.

Follow-up
Look at what you expect the outcomes to be for children as a result of the planned activities. Do they, in turn, represent a balance of experiences? Adjust your timetable as necessary.

Starting the day with talk

Objectives
To generate interest immediately children arrive in the classroom and to promote language and discussion between children or between adults and children.

What you need
Anything new to the classroom such as a vase of flowers or twigs or a new toy, book or resource, and a specially designated place just inside the entrance to the classroom where such items can always be located.

What to do
Place the object in a prominent place, carefully displayed, in time for the first

child's arrival. Tell the children and accompanying adults that it is there to talk about. Insist it is left there until all the children have had the opportunity to see and talk about it. Allow the children to handle it during the day and use it for discussion in an odd two minutes.

Variation
Where there is a current topic, it is useful to have an appropriate item related to the topic. For example, if the topic is 'hands', a pair of brightly coloured mittens or gloves might be a useful starter.

Changing library books

Objectives
To enable parents to share the choosing of library books with children and to ensure that books are safely returned.

What you need
Thin coloured card to make a book ticket pocket for each child, a display board, a book loan system for families.

What to do
Think about your current topic or focus, which might, for example, be food. Draw and cut out some small food shapes which are slightly larger than a library ticket, ensuring you have matching pairs which can be stapled together round the edge, leaving the top open to produce a food 'pocket'. Write the child's name on the food. Mount the 'food' attractively on to the display board.

Encourage the parents and children when they arrive at the beginning of a session to choose a book to take home, placing the ticket in their child's 'food pocket'.

What to do
Cut the card into long rectangles (about 30×90cm) to make large signs with huge letters. Use the string to hang them from the ceiling over specific areas or activities in the class base, for example, Sand Area, Water Play, Big Bricks, Stories and Poems. Add pictorial cues or even real life cues, for example, hang a bucket and spade under the Sand Area sign. Encourage the children to look around the room before selecting where to go.

Dealing with safety issues

Objective
To ensure children understand, in a fun way, that keeping safe is a vital part of the class base as well as everyday life.

What you need
Real, or pictures of, potentially dangerous items which may be found in the class base or home, for example, a boiling kettle, plugs, craft knives, pointed scissors, a cooker, woodwork tools, matches.

What to do
Talk to the children about each item. What is it? What does it do? Is it safe for children to use on their own? What are its 'danger' points? How should it be safely used. It is vital that children are not just protected from danger but are also given a responsibility for considering their own and others' safety.

Follow-up
Large outline drawings or pictures of the objects could be displayed with mapping strings to the danger points from a model or cut-out of a child or a child's hands. This is a good way to introduce the words 'danger' and 'stop'.

I don't know where to go!

Objective
To label the areas of the classroom clearly and encourage children to look and choose.

What you need
Large, stiff card, stout string, cut-out letters or letter templates, thick felt-tipped pens.

Encouraging positive behaviour patterns

Objective
To work towards ensuring children understand the reasons for, and the enjoyable results of, behaving appropriately in the class base.

What you need
Dolls, animals or puppets, suitable 'props' (for example, if getting dirty is to be discussed, at least one toy should have dirty clothes).

What to do
Decide which aspects of unacceptable behaviour you wish to concentrate on. Your decision could be the result of some 'incident' which has occurred recently and may include:
● fighting;
● making someone else cry or be unhappy;
● pushing other children;
● standing on someone's models;
● scribbling on a book or damaging something precious.
(Be careful not to include events which were accidental.)

Act out a scene where two of the toys start a fight, push each other around or trample on a model. Discuss with the children what is happening. Allow them to ask questions of the 'toys' about cause and effect. Then allow them to offer potential solutions and discuss what rules might be necessary were this to happen in their class base. This could begin a collection of 'Our Rules' which the children can illustrate, display or make into a book.

Variations
● Children can role play scenes of good and bad behaviour as part of story time.
● Pictures of children and adults doing different things can be used in a similar way to the toy people representations. Mount a display which includes children's transcribed comments on their behaviour.
● Read a story about bad behaviour, for example, *The Tale of Georgie Grub* by J. Willis, and ask for children's comments on the behaviour and its effects.

What can you hear?

Objective
To allow children to experiment with what it means to be noisy and quiet, and to learn when and where these are appropriate within the class area.

What you need
A tape-recorder.

What to do
Tape the sounds of children in various areas of the early years setting, such as in the playground, in the role play area, while listening to a story and while reading themselves.
Let the children listen to the sounds and try to identify what is happening and

where. Ask them to think about which ones they consider to be 'noisy' and which ones are 'quiet'. When do they like or need to be noisy or quiet? If one child wants to be noisy and others quiet, how can this be resolved and what needs to happen?

Follow-up
Read *Nicky's Noisy Night* by H. Ziefert or *Goodnight Owl* by P. Hutchins to show the children they are not the only ones who make a noise!

We don't do that here!

Objective
To allow adults and children to think through the rules of the class base.

What you need
Group time for talking and decision-making — staff first, then children.

What to do
Talk together as a staff. What implicit or explicit rules do you apply in the class base? Why? Are they all necessary?

Should there be additions or amendments? The old saying 'rules were made to be broken' applies nowhere more so than in schools, so try to have as few as possible (not more than about six).

Ask the children about rules and what they are. Do they have any rules in the class base? Why do we have rules?

Follow-up
Make a collection of children's pictures about rules in the class base and mount these into a book.

Mix and (mis)match

Objective
To consider how far materials and play opportunities can be extended through relaxing 'rules' about keeping resources separate from each other.

What you need
Plastic mushroom pegs, straws, compost, a variety of small objects such as pipe-cleaners and LEGO, water and sand trays, cartridge paper, wax crayons, pencils, charcoal.

What to do

We tend to give particular materials specific labels in relation to use, for example, mushroom pegs are for making patterns on plastic or wooden holed trays, sand trays contain sand and sand equipment, and so on. This can, however, significantly restrict creativity! Here are some suggestions as to how to mix materials:

• Allow the children to put a mass of mushroom pegs in the water bath and watch what happens (some will float but others will, mysteriously, sink). Blowing them around through a straw, trying to get the floaters to sink and trying to get them to 'stick' on the end of the straw by (careful) sucking are all good scientific learning experiences.

• Do crayons write underwater? Let children push some cartridge paper to the bottom of the water tray and then try to write on it with wax crayons, pencil crayons, pencils and charcoal. What are the effects?

• Fill the sand tray with prepared compost and hide some objects in there such as pipe-cleaners and small bricks. Let the children try to find the objects by feeling for them and ask them to guess what they are by their 'feel'. Partially sighted children are excellent at this and enjoy being able to 'shine' with their peers.

Follow-up

Where materials have become soiled, let the children clean them in a bowl of warm soapy water, or adapt the water tray for this purpose.

Special activity cloth

Objective

To make a particular activity or task 'special' and encourage children to want to work on a different activity.

What you need

A tablecloth, preferably plain but bright (primary colours are ideal).

What to do

Lay out the cloth on the work table before placing the necessary materials on top in an attractive display. The introduction of a bright red surface (to perhaps an otherwise fairly mundane table) will bring them flocking in!

Follow-up

• The cloth could also be spread on the floor for special floor activities.
• Individual mats could be made available to children so that they can decide whether the activity they have chosen is 'special' or particularly important to them. These could be fabric or place mats made from off-cuts, pieces of floor covering or left-over floor tiles.

Where is my milk?

Objective
To use drinks- and snack-times as a reading opportunity.

What you need
Plastic squeezy bottles, thin elastic thread, a waterproof pen, a fine-hole punch.

What to do
Allow the children to choose when to have a drink as they usually intuitively know when they need a 'break'.

A suitably clean table area or shelf can act as a 'drinks machine' which children and/or adults can set out early in the session. Bottles, packets or beakers can be clustered into number groups, sorted by colour or by types of drinks.

The event can be used to encourage the reading of each other's names by making a label for each child in the class. Cut the plastic bottles into strips and write a name on the plain side of each piece.

Punch two holes in each top corner and secure sufficient elastic thread across the top of the label to hang it round the neck of a milk bottle or carton. You may wish to make the reading task easier by writing names in different colours so that the child at least knows that his or her name is, say, one of the five red ones.

Variations
• If you have morning and afternoon, or full-time and part-time children, use different coloured plastic bottle labels as a way of making the task easier.
• If the children have name labels, these could be used as a matching activity with the milk labels.

Home corner routines

Objective
To change the type and range of play available in the standard home corner set-up.

What you need
A list of standard home corner materials.

What to do
Think about the establishment of *one room* instead of trying to pack several rooms into one home corner. Let the area become only a kitchen or sitting room or bedroom. This will significantly change the type of play and the children can be encouraged to sort the relevant equipment and think about different rooms in their own homes.

Variation
Where there are two or more three-sided home corner structures available, each could be set side-by-side as different rooms.

Materials and resources

Chapter three

One of the main aims of early years education has always been to engender in children a sense of independence and autonomy (Bruce, 1987; Fisher, 1990), allied to which must be opportunities for making personal choices about activities and materials. For example, how can children choose a suitable medium for reproducing their image of 'a rainy day' if they have not had the opportunity to explore a range of techniques and materials and the effects they produce?

Sensible choices can only be made if three main factors prevail: first, the organisation of materials allows for their ready access and replacement by children and adults, including those with special needs or disabilities; second, children are taught how and *why* they should access and replace materials properly; third, children have the opportunity to explore a wide range of techniques and materials appropriate to different outcomes.

Choice, paradoxically, also requires limitations. Young children can be overwhelmed by the variety of options in the early years setting, with the result that they either choose to watch, or rest fleetingly like butterflies at each port of call!

The classroom environment and its material and resource organisation offer in themselves a most relevant and purposeful part of children's learning: the biggest books can only live on the deepest, tallest shelves; the scissors are dangerous if stored with their points upwards; and the cookery equipment must be kept in a special cupboard where it will not get dusty. All of these and many more offer real and useful learning experiences to children, as well as ensuring a safe and pleasant environment for everyone.

What shall we put where?

Objective
To decide where to store materials and resources for ease of access by adults and children alike.

What you need
Two separate lists, one of expendable materials and one of play resources regularly available in the class base (photocopied for all the staff), a location plan and storage cut-outs (see 'What goes where?', page 11).

What to do
In a staff meeting decide as a group on suitable classifications for materials and resources, for example, painting equipment, dough equipment or science and technology play, language and literacy. (These should be related to the decisions you made in Chapter One regarding class areas or bays.)

Independently look down your lists and add a classification suitable to each item. For example, large blocks could be classified LC (large construction) and M (mathematical orientation). A home corner area might be classified as L (language oriented) or even OL (mainly oral language) but with DT (design/technology) capability.

Share your classifications, refine them, group them accordingly and decide roughly where each item should go.

Using the location plan of designated areas or bays, your storage cut-outs and your knowledge of the size of equipment, assign the materials according to their classification and the available storage.

Follow-up
Transfer your final product into the real class area! Label everything appropriately. This activity will no doubt lead to the identification of need for different resources or for additional storage, both of which are useful to know when next offered opportunities for buying equipment.

Labelling

Objective
To ensure children and adults will know where to access and return classroom resources.

What you need
Pictures from the packages in which materials arrived or from suppliers' catalogues or drawings of the materials, cardboard, clear self-adhesive plastic, scissors, sticky-tape.

What to do
Depending upon the size of the material and its ultimate storage location, cut out two suitably sized pictures of the material, mount them on card (colour-coded if wished) and cover them with clear self-adhesive plastic. Attach one of these newly made labels to the storage space and the other to the appropriate container. Children will then be able to practise matching as they learn to tidy away after themselves!

Variations
• You could take photographs of the materials and have a double set processed – one set for the material and one for the storage space.
• Children could be asked to draw (or draw round) some of the basic materials like scissors and pencils. Exactly similar second copies can be achieved through photocopying.
• Where no picture is available, the resource could be coded with a shape or symbol which is then attached to both the item and the storage area.
• Written labels (in English or other mother tongues) can also be added or substituted for pictures.

Shadow labelling

Objective
To allow children and adults to identify the location of materials by shape and colour and to see when an item is missing.

What you need
Coloured card, clear self-adhesive plastic, Blu-Tack, pens.

What to do
If the item – such as a pencil pot or scissor box – sits neatly on a shelf or counter top, draw around the base of the object. If the object stands next to a wall, the outline shape can be cut from card and mounted behind where it will be placed. Use card of the same colour as the object, cover it for durability and fix it onto the relevant surface. Stand the object on top.

Variation
The shapes can be cut from black card as 'shadows' if you want to make the replacing exercise slightly more difficult.

Woodwork tools

Objective
To create a special storage area for tools where their replacement can be monitored and sensible access made available.

What you need
For the board: a piece of pegboard, four wooden battens to make an edging for the frame (at least 3cm deep, 2cm wide), two squares of 0.5cm-plywood cut diagonally to give four 90° angle triangles, four metal ear-plates, 3cm-nails, four rawlplugs and screws, an electric drill. For the tools: cardboard, a black felt-tipped pen, Blu-Tack, metal 's' hooks (these can be bought or made from 10cm-strips of wire coathanger) one for each tool, strong string.

What to do
Back the edges of your pegboard with the wooden battens, one along each side. Stiffen and stabilise each corner with a plywood triangle. Fix the ear-plates to the top and bottom edge, about 10cm in from the side edge and mount it onto the wall, using the drill, rawlplugs and screws.

Next draw around the tools to make a shadow outline on the cardboard. Cut these out and attach them to the board with Blu-Tack. Then attach an 's' hook to the board so that the tool hangs directly down from it over the outline. Some tools, such as hammers, may need to hang from a loop of string.

Variation
Tool outlines could be colour coded according to their use, for example, whether they are for hammering or drilling.

Where can we find it?

Objectives
To help children who are newcomers in your class to find and replace materials easily. To help children see the benefits of having everything in its place.

What you need
All your materials and resources located in appropriate places and all labelled as discussed above.

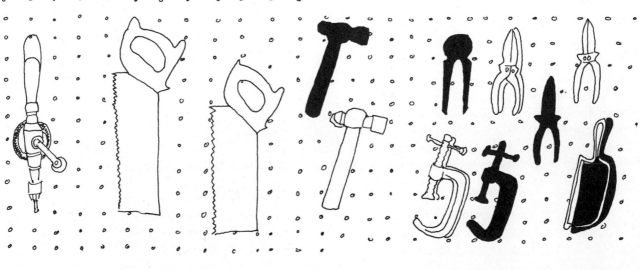

What to do

Tell the children that you are going to play a special game to help them find all the things they need. Ask if anyone is clever enough to say where the scissors, for example, are kept. Select a child and let them find the item and bring it to show all the other children. Then ask, 'Is there anyone clever enough to show us where to put the scissors back?' Select a child to replace the item. Do this with a few pieces of equipment at a time until the children can readily locate the things they will need.

Follow-up

This can be done with any materials and should be continued during the year as new items are acquired.

I did it my way!

Objective

To explore different techniques with children so they can make choices as to how they represent their ideas and feelings through pictures and models.

What you need

Pastels, paints, watercolour pencils and any other drawing and painting materials used to produce different effects.

What to do

Show the children a different drawing or painting technique, at least once a week. Demonstrate how the medium works — with water, without water, on different papers, to make a misty picture, a watery picture and so on. See Gentle (1993) for ideas and media. The objective is not that children should follow exactly what you do but that they should have the opportunity to explore the media for themselves. They often have their own ideas for techniques.

Follow-up

Do the same with tactile media such as dough or clay, pointing out their different properties, their stability, strength and the ways in which they change when made wet or dry.

What shall we do today?

Objective

To encourage children to make choices based on predetermined ideas of what they would like to do.

What you need

Pictures, photographs or drawings of classroom situations.

What to do

Instead of putting out play materials and resources prior to the session and then having children wander around the classroom trying to decide what to do, use the photographs or drawings to make 'decision cards'. Children who find choice difficult can be given a limited selection of options, while others can be given a wider choice. Having selected the card appropriate to the task of their choice, the children then go off to retrieve the items they need.

Follow-up

This can be extended to a sequence of activities. Let the children make first, second and even third choices of what they want to do during the session. Pictures of other children would also help those who need to decide on a peer friend to play with.

Sorting 'found' materials

Objective
To make the storage and retrieval of modelling and collage materials a learning experience for children and easy for everyone.

What you need
Large storage crates or coloured grocery boxes, miscellaneous materials such as household boxes and fabrics.

What to do
With the children, sort the boxes into recognisable shapes. Sort the fabrics into either textures or colours. Place each set in its own labelled crate or box and store. Children will quickly learn the names, particularly if a representation of the shape, texture or a patch of colour is used as a label.

Variation
Anything can be sorted in this way. If boxes take up too much space then strong, plastic carrier bags are useful in the short term.

Storing 'found' materials

Objective
To store potentially large and cumbersome resources in a limited space but still be able to use them readily.

What you need
Packaging such as cereal boxes, cardboard tubes and chocolate boxes.

What to do
Let each child open out a package into its original shape. The containers can then be stored folded flat. When the containers are to be used, most can be turned inside out to make painting easier and re-formed. Young children will want to do this re-forming and painting as an activity in itself.

Simple pencil pots

Objective
To make inexpensive, sturdy and attractive storage for pencils, brushes and rulers.

What you need
Thick cardboard tubes of the type used in carpet rolls, thick cardboard, strong glue, gloss paint, sandpaper, a saw, a craft knife.

What to do
To hold standard pencils use the saw or craft knife (dependent on thickness) to cut the tube into 10cm lengths. Using the end of a tube as a template, draw and cut out cardboard circles and glue these on firmly for the bases. When dry, sandpaper the edges lightly to take away any roughness and then paint them with at least two layers of gloss paint.

For wax or small crayons the tube should be cut into shallower 6cm pieces. For rulers and longer items 15–18cm is more appropriate.

Variation
Granular food products now come in cardboard cylinders which are easily painted with gloss paint or covered in sticky-backed plastic and make equally good storage pots.

Colour-sorted crayons

Objective
To ensure that wax crayons remain consistent in colour (pale colours often streak darker colours onto paper after being stored with darker ones), and to encourage colour-sorting.

What you need
Crayon pots or trays in different colours, wax (or pencil) crayons, spare crayon pots.

What to do
Put all the red crayons together in a red pot, green in the green pot, and so on (the children can do this). Insist that they are permanently stored like this.

When the children need the crayons, encourage them to take an empty pot and make conscious choices as to the colours needed. After use, the crayons are returned and sorted by colour into their original storage pots.

Variation
Used paintbrushes can also be stored in this way. Colour words can be added to the pots.

The squirrel instinct

Objective
To make use of what could otherwise be thrown away.

What you need
An assortment of scrap materials that might otherwise be thrown away.

What to do
Use any of the following ideas for recycling junk material.
- Film tubs make excellent sealable glue pots.
- Thick polystyrene blocks, cut into neat cuboids with a craft knife, make scissor-, pencil- and paintbrush-holders. Simply heat a thick knitting needle and pierce the block at regular intervals (with scissors the gaps must allow for the spread of the handles).
- Plastic sweet jars make excellent storage for a whole range of items.
- Vinyl flooring offcuts or spare tiles make washable Plasticine or dough mats.
- Large, handled washing powder boxes make strong and durable storage for hundreds of items.

Sorting our odds and ends

Objective
To give variation, purpose and relevance to sorting activities.

What you need
A collection of (probably discarded) clean household items including ties, socks, gloves, shoe laces, ribbon, lace left-overs, buttons, beads.

What to do
Let the children sort the items in a variety of ways, for example, by size, colour, shape, pattern, pairings, length or diameter.

Follow-up
The items could be sorted into 'stock' for a suitable shop, for example, Sock Shop, Tie Rack. An 'odds-and-evens' shop is a novel and useful idea as odd socks are something children will have heard parents complaining about!

Using paper offcuts

Objective
To make use of all paper offcuts.

What you need
Any offcuts of paper (including strips, squares, odd shapes, triangles), scissors.

What to do
Think what representation comes to your mind, or the children's, for each offcut. Perhaps fish, fruit, houses or animals spring to mind. Cut the paper into the relevant form, with as little waste as possible. Store these shapes near the drawing, writing or painting areas to stimulate ideas when the children are at work in them.

Variation
Fabrics can be treated similarly. Cutting fabric into a dress- or trouser-shape often prompts a collage.

The story board

Objective
To create a board for a story sequence.

What you need
Four or six equally sized pieces of plywood about 30×30×0.5cm, a piece of felt, hessian or other material with a rough surface (about 65cm deep × 1.25m long for four panels or 65cm × 1.9m for six panels), sewing thread, a sewing machine, sandpaper, picture cut-outs for a story, adhesive.

What to do
Make a long tube out of the material by sewing along the longest edge and up one side. Slide in the first piece of plywood right to the sewn end and then sew down the edge to hold it in place. Slide in the second piece of plywood and sew securely, then repeat the process until all the plywood is used up (Figure 1). Sew the end to hold it all in place. You can now use this as a display board, standing it upright, in concertina form or a U-shape, or lie it down on the floor.

Stick sandpaper on to the back of the cut-outs. They will adhere to the surface of the story board and be readily moved. As the board is exactly similar on both sides, two groups of children can be working at the same time.

Variations
• If plywood is not available, very thick card or strawboard will do but may not be quite as long-lasting.
• Single- or double-panel story boards can be made in different sizes for individual child use.

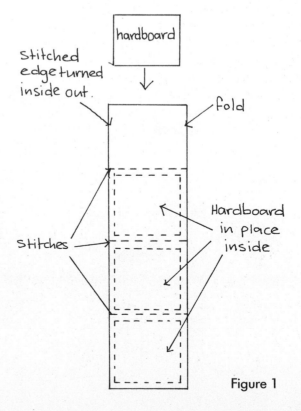

Figure 1

Story secrets in the bag!

Objective
To add a calming and satisfying 'ritual' to story time.

What you need
A cloth bag containing objects related to the story you are going to tell.

What to do
Talk to the children in a mysterious way about the bag and what might be inside! Slowly draw out the objects and ask the children about them. Try to get some prediction, potential story vocabulary and so on from them. Hold each object as if it were very special and when discussion subsides, gently begin to tell the story.

Follow-up
A book to read as well as an object could be placed inside a bag for the children themselves. Encourage them to go through the same story 'rituals'.

Beginnings, endings and special times

Chapter four

Among the most difficult times of the day in early years settings are the beginnings and endings. Children's separation from parents and carers at the beginning of the session can be traumatic on all sides but having a well-organised, homely and welcoming environment (as discussed in Chapter two) can go some way to ensuring that it is a stress-free time.

A smooth transition from home to school and back again is vital for all those concerned as it is a key time for communication (McLean, 1991). Each morning everything needed for the day ahead must be ready so that time can be given to children and carers as they arrive. All those events, such as birthdays, new babies, special festivals, visitors or holidays, which link home life and school life, need to be anticipated.

At different times in the school day the focus of events change and, if not handled smoothly, they can cause anxiety for some children. Tidy-away time with young children has long been the new teacher's nightmare, but, as discussed in Chapter three, having labelled, accessible resources and playing 'tidy-up' games help tremendously.

Lining up has a long history of potential time-wasting, for teachers and children, and in many classrooms it seems the prime time for adults' nagging and children fidgeting and even fighting! It may be necessary but does not have to be a necessary evil! In this chapter, a range of ideas for making transitions easier is explored.

You're welcome!

Objective
To ensure children and adults will feel welcome in their new environment by outlining some of its similarities to and differences from previous experiences.

What you need
A home-made book or photograph album, pictures of children at playgroup, at home, in the park, in school, in the playground, in assembly, a loans system.

What to do
Make up a 'Welcome Book'. It should have two sections:
• Before you came to school . . .
• Now you are in school . . .
Each section will have photographs, with suitable captions, of what children will have done prior to coming to school and what they will do in school. It is best if the 'before school' photographs are of the actual children in their real settings.

Captions should be worded in such a way as to both value the experiences and encourage children to see that differences will be small but exciting!

Organise a loans system so that parents and carers (usually from the pre-school setting) can borrow the book to share with their children.

Variation
A home-produced video, with booklet, showing the same kind of activities is more time-consuming to make but provides a greater 'feel' for each situation.

Making the register fun

Objectives
To involve parents and children in registering their arrival and to help children identify their own names.

What you need
Coloured card, paint, Velcro, glue, a pen, scissors, a box or packet.

What to do
Make a large cut-out of a tree. Draw the outline of a leaf on the tree for each child in the class.

Write the name of each child twice, once on the tree cut-out and once on a separate leaf made from card. Stick Velcro to each leaf outline and each separate leaf. Let the children hunt for their names as a game, pulling them off and sticking them back on again.

When the children are familiar with their own name tell them and the accompanying adult that this is to be the 'Register Tree'. Place the separate leaves in a box or packet near to where the children enter and encourage each child and adult to find the child's name and place it on the tree to show the teacher that they have arrived. The teacher can transfer the information to the formal register while the children are getting on with their activities.

Variation
Almost any cut-out would do but it needs to be straightforward and robust and could be usefully covered with clear self-adhesive plastic. In winter it could be icicles hanging from a wall; in summer it could be petals on a row of flowers.

I'm staying dinners!

Objectives
To vary the way in which children's attendance is recorded and to give them some responsibility for what they will do during the day.

What you need
A cut-out drawing or photograph of each child, card, glue, a pen, two pictures of food, two large circles (either plastic hoops or drawn on card).

What to do
Mount the photographs on separate pieces of card. Label each circle with a picture of food, but cross through one of the labels to indicate 'no food'.

Spread the photographs face-up on the carpet and call children a few at a time to find their photograph and place it in the appropriate circle to show whether or not they are staying for dinner.

Follow-up
The availability of the dinner menu (in pictorial and written form) offers adults and children the opportunity to discuss likes, dislikes and possibilities!

Time to begin

Objectives
To provide a calm and organised start to the session or day for adults and children and to help children, and the adults who bring them, have a calm, sharing period before the adult withdraws.

What you need
The class base, or an area in it, organised in such a way that children can come in and start an activity without direction from the adults.

What to do
Set up the activity in an interesting way and direct the children to it, thus freeing you to communicate with parents and carers. You might set up a book display, play materials or a colouring activity. There may be another adult in the room who can draw the children towards the activity.

Communication (or treasure) boxes

Objectives
To allow for written communication between home and school without immediate contact between adults and to provide storage for the children's 'treasures'.

What you need
A stout shoe box for each child, glue, gloss paint, scissors, short treasury tags, a hole punch, labels with each child's name.

What to do
Create a bank of boxes by stacking and gluing them in an attractive format so that one end of each shoe box becomes the 'face'. Cut a 'door' into each face leaving one side attached as a hinge. Punch a hole in the door and in the frame and insert a treasury tag as a closure device (see Figure 1). To strengthen the stack, paint the whole lot with gloss paint and add a label showing each child's name to the doors. Decorate it attractively. Place the stack in a suitable position in the classroom.

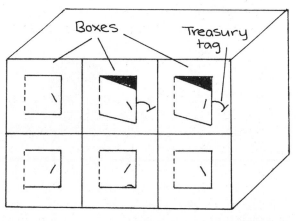

Figure 1

Let the children and parents learn about their individual 'treasure box' and how to use it as a source of communication. Classroom adults (and parents) need to remember to check if there are any notes! Children can learn to roll up pictures and place them in the boxes during the day.

Variations
• The boxes can be made into smaller banks and scattered around the room so that children and parents do not all converge on the same place during the morning.
• Stacking in pyramids also looks attractive and the bank can be mounted on a wall.
• If money is available a more permanent wooden structure may be a good idea.

NB These boxes should be within the class base rather than outside it for safety reasons.

Two-minute fillers

Objective
To effectively fill those short moments at the end of a session.

What you need
Paper, an easel, pens, familiar objects and toys.

What to do
There are many quick activities which have a good learning basis, many of which are very obvious like counting rhymes, poetry, nursery rhymes, songs and so on. Here are just a few more ideas:
• If children are learning left and right, using a large sheet of paper on an easel, take a line for a walk with a big pen,

asking individual children whether to continue the line moving left or right.

• You could pre-draw a maze and ask the children to tell you which way to turn. (If you cover it with sticky-backed plastic and use a water-based pen, your maze could be used over and over again.)

• Draw two lines and ask which is the shortest and which is the longest or draw three lines – short, shorter and shortest.

• Draw a quick pattern or sequence and get individual children to come up and copy it, or let them draw their own for another child.

• Quick number stories: 'There are three apples on a tree, two fall off, how many are left?'

• Start a sentence: 'The children played with matches and . . .', 'The dog was digging in the garden and . . .', allowing the children to suggest an ending.

• Say 'A cat' and ask the children to add a description, for example, 'A naughty cat'. This can be continued by children adding descriptions until they cannot remember them all: 'A naughty, black cat', 'A naughty, black, furry cat', and so on.

• Children can sit in a circle and pass round a teddy, doll or toy car and each one has to find something to say about the object. If children are too slow they pass it on and think about something to say when it comes round again.

• 'Different bits': this can be used for books, objects, own bodies, computer, plants – almost anything. The adult points to a part of the object and asks children to name it; the younger the child the simpler the parts.

Silence signals

Objective
To offer an alternative to the use of the adult's voice in the midst of activities when it is time to end the session.

What you need
Any small instrument with a high- or very low-pitched sound, for example, an Indian bell, small cymbal, triangle, deep drum, beater.

What to do
Play statue games during outdoor or hall sessions using the instrument, ensuring that children stand really still when they hear the sound.

When children are sufficiently confident that they can respond quickly, tell them this sound will, in future, become the special 'stop and listen' sound within the class base. Whenever they hear the sound, it will be to tell them that something different is going to happen.

Follow-up
The instrument will need to be changed periodically to sustain interest.

41

Are you sitting comfortably?

Objective
To think through the needs of a story-telling session in order to ensure all children have the opportunity to listen without disturbance.

What you need
A little time to monitor the carpet areas, or wherever story-telling takes place.

What to do
Think about your story area. Is the carpet fraying and will children pick at it? Are there certain cushions or chairs which children constantly bicker over? Are there things around the edges which children will want to fiddle with? Are the children sitting too close together and thereby encouraged to mess around with each other's clothing?

All these are potentially disruptive in story time and repair or relocation needs careful consideration. Where cushions and chairs are the problem, is there some kind of rota system you could work out with the children? Where children fuss with each other's hair or clothing, would a circular seating arrangement offer a solution? If the area is too small could some children sit on nearby chairs? If the storage of items around the carpet area causes problems, could these be turned round to face outwards instead of inwards?

Having something to focus on such as an artefact, puppet or toy often encourages concentration and stillness.

Follow-up
If a child constantly interrupts the story, ask what they would rather do. Perhaps he or she would prefer to draw pictures. If so allow the child to do so each story time so the rest of the children can listen without disturbance.

Let's have a party!

Objective
To celebrate any special occasion — the birth of a baby, a particular cultural or religious festival, to round the term off well — or just to do something different.

What you need
Party items such as food, squash and paper plates, materials for making invitations, hats, mats and serviettes.

What to do
Send letters home to parents (children could do these) telling them what the celebration is for and asking them to make a contribution. You can tailor the contribution to what you know the family may be able to provide.

Get the children to plan the party including day, time, invitations, food, special hats, placemats, serviettes and so on. They should then design and make necessary items, send invitations, plan the table layout and, when the day arrives, do a count-down on the clock and build up to the big event.

Depending on how many children are involved and how many adults are available this could take just one day or may be spread over several. Food ingredients could be bought so the children themselves can make up recipes.

Variations
• A simple squash and biscuit party could be held each time a child has a birthday. A healthy alternative would be a fruit and nut party.
• This kind of celebration is particularly relevant for different cultural and religious festivals, particularly as the food made and eaten will be varied.

Let's celebrate a birthday!

Objective
To make children feel special on their birthdays.

What you need
Material (hessian, gingham, poplin), embroidery threads, felt pieces.

What to do
Use the material to make a back to fit over a standard classroom chair. Cut a large '4', '5' or '6' and write or embroider a birthday greeting on the fabric. (You will need one cover for each of the age groups whose birthdays you are likely to celebrate.)

The child's birthday is best celebrated early in the day, he or she sitting in the special chair for the usual celebration, and the child can then use this special chair for the rest of the day.

Variation
A birthday cushion could be made for the chair seat in a similar style.

A writing board for communication

Objective
For children to learn that communication is a purposeful activity in which they play a major part.

What you need
A low-level display board, a large caption such as 'I want to tell you about . . .', paper, pencils, crayons, Blu-Tack.

What to do
Tell the children that the display board is for passing messages on to each other. They must be allowed to 'write' in whatever way suits them and pictorial information is equally useful. They must, however, write their own name on the picture and also write the name of the person who is to receive the message.

Variations
• Children could tape-record their messages. In different languages this makes for interesting listening!
• Old envelopes can be reused by putting sticky labels over them; coloured labels add another opportunity for children to identify their own message.
• Parental involvement could also be encouraged if children create messages or pictures at home, adding captions in other written languages with help from members of the family.

Save the hamster!

Objective
To assuage children's anxieties during fire drills and show that all living things will be safe!

What you need
Nominated people – adults or children – who will carry the class pets outside in fire drills or should the real thing happen.

What to do
Children are often very upset during and following fire drills, fearing that classroom pets will be burned. Much anxiety can be saved by ensuring someone has the clear responsibility for taking pets outside. A good idea is to have an adult and nominated child responsible.

Follow-up
• A story about the class hamster, telling of its likes and dislikes, could include an episode about being taken out during a fire drill.
• Talking about fire drills and their purpose and making up or reading relevant stories helps children come to terms with their anxiety. Having a fire station area or a 'fire week' also helps.

Making an exit

Objective
To make coming to and going from the class base more orderly.

What you need
Clear ideas and clear instructions for the children about leaving and entering the class base.

What to do
Think about the ways in which children leave the class base. Do they line up at the door or in a certain place? Does this regularly cause a fuss? Do children continually jostle each other? Do they stand and fiddle with classroom equipment?

It is far better to have children ready to leave the area in smaller groups and then to ask them, group by group, to walk out calmly. Look around the base for spaces where groups can congregate. If necessary make these the 'home bases' for certain named children, so that you can split up those who find it difficult to socialise with each other.

Variation
Get the children to stand on the carpet prior to leaving the classroom and then allow them to leave according to various categories, such as by the colour of their sweaters or shoes.

Going home time

Objective
To match children with their parents or carers at the end of the day.

What you need
An additional adult is helpful.

What to do
Discourage children from leaping up as soon as they see their own parent or carer. Explain the need for you to be sure they leave safely and with the right person.

Children should be responsible for collecting and putting on their own coats so that they are physically ready for the collecting adult and can leave the class base quickly and easily. Having the children seated together in one area not too far from the door, ensures they and you can see the 'match-up' of adult and child taking place. Here are some ideas for a safe match-up:

• Children's items to be taken home can be stored in boldly named bags, in a box by the door, and when the collecting adults arrive, they can find the bag for their child and hold it up so that you, and the children, can see whom they have come to collect.

• A nursery adult can stand by the door or entrance to the base, orally collect the name of the child and then call it out. Another nursery adult can check each child has all necessary possessions and leaves the area to greet the collecting adult.

• Particularly if there is only one teacher, encourage the children to think about the person collecting them by giving a description: 'I'm thinking of a mummy/daddy/granny/friend with blonde hair, glasses and wearing a red coat.' Correct identification allows the children to be 'released'.

• The parent or carer and child can each be given one half of a picture card. The adult shows their half of the card when they arrive at the end of the session and the child matches this up with the other half.

Organising for play

Chapter five

Children learn in a variety of important ways through play and, in making sound provision for play, we are making sound provision for learning (Moyles, 1989; Garvey, 1991; Smilansky and Shefataya, 1990).

Particular kinds of play lend themselves to different forms of learning. Dramatic, 'pretend' play enhances intellectual development and language performance. Constructional play offers opportunities for problem solving, designing, making and the development of technical competency. Sand, water and other tactile play investigations enhance scientific and mathematical understanding. Physical and outdoor play provide opportunities for gross motor mastery and physical and social performance. Good organisation allows these forms of play to be readily available.

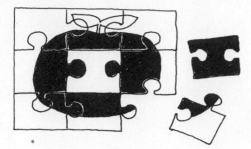

It can also be useful to do the exercise with individual categories of play materials such as jigsaw puzzles and language games, examining them in terms of difficulty.

Varying the play

Objectives
To show children how play spaces can have different uses and to make everyday things more special.

What you need
Empty sand or water trays, or large kitchen trays, constructional toys, Playpeople, twigs, lollipop sticks, Plasticine, garden soil, paint.

What to do
Put small constructional toys, Playpeople, vehicles and small buildings into an empty water or sand tray. You could add twigs for trees and lollipop sticks in Plasticine for signs. Sterilised soil could be added to the tray with Playpeople builders and diggers. (Garden soil can be sterilised in a microwave. Spread it evenly on a plastic tray and put it in on a high setting for two or three minutes.)

Old kitchen trays can be plainly painted or can have basic scenes, such as grass and water, painted onto them for prompting certain kinds of constructional uses or mini-world stories.

Variation
A cloth can make ordinary toys seem special (see 'Special activity cloth', page 25). Each play material could have its own special cloth, dyed or painted with particular scenes such as fields for a farm, sand and the seaside or different rooms in a house.

What do we need?

Objectives
To help you decide whether your provision for play is sufficiently varied and to encourage the careful ordering of additional play materials.

What you need
Coloured pens, paper.

What to do
Decide on some categories for play materials (Kirklees Metropolitan Council, 1985), for example, large construction, small construction, jigsaws, mini-worlds, stimulus area, pretend, creative, scientific, mathematical play. Next, list your own base's play materials, writing them into the appropriate category. (It is difficult to do this with absolute accuracy as play materials have multi-curricular purposes but you need only to be as specific as you yourself believe appropriate!)

Gaps in provision are now both obvious and, if money is available, easily remedied.

Follow-up
It may be possible to make some items, such as the cardboard play blocks described on page 50. Jumble sales can provide good but inexpensive items.

Alternative storage

Objective
To find alternative uses for storage items to benefit the children's play.

What you need
Book boxes, trolleys and any other storage equipment.

What to do
Think about changing the storage of equipment in order to regenerate the children's interest in particular materials. As an example, the storage of LEGO in the four sections of a wooden 'book box' on legs offers opportunities for the LEGO to be sorted into plain bricks, trees and signs, vehicles and wheels and specific accessories. Book boxes can be purchased or you can make one by gluing together and gloss-painting four shallow grocery boxes.

Old two- and three-tray trolleys allow more mix-and-match opportunities, such as with Plasticine or DUPLO.

'Gender-free' play clothes

Objective
To have dressing-up clothes available which are, as far as possible, free of gender bias and flexible in their use.

What you need
Paper, a pencil, scissors, pieces of washable material, tapes, ribbon, Velcro, sewing threads, a sewing machine, bits and pieces for decoration.

What to do
Make a standard 'tabard' pattern out of paper to fit the age of a child in your base. Use this to cut out the fabric, the colour of which will determine what it might end up as; for example, white with a red cross could be for a nurse or doctor, silver with heraldic emblems could be for a knight, while browns and greys could make animal outfits. Attach any desirable decorations and side fastenings.

Variation
Equally simple but effective is a basic type of 'apron' pattern to make cloaks which, if made about twice the size of a standard apron waist, can be worn round the shoulders, chest or waist to be representative of almost anything the child wishes.

Simple play masks

Objective
To create simple masks which do not obscure children's faces.

What you need
Thin A3 cardboard or cartridge paper, pen, scissors, glue, bits and pieces for decoration, thin elastic, a stapler.

What to do
Fold the card lengthways and draw half a face of an animal, working from the folded side (see Figure 1). Do not bother about the ears at this stage. Simple, long and thin shapes will make the faces of mice or crocodiles, short and stubby shapes will make bears, cats, monkeys and so on. Use the remaining card to cut out ear shapes or, for frogs, large eyes, and for birds, head feathers. Mount the pieces together into a three-dimensional shape by pushing the ear pieces down into the fold, and gluing or stapling them in place (see Figure 2). Decorate them as appropriate (children can easily do this) and add the elastic as a chin strap.

The mask sits readily on top of the child's head so that they can talk and see very clearly while still representing a character of their choice.

Follow-up
Masks are a useful device for acting out assembly stories.

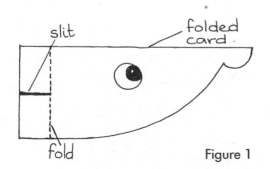

Figure 1

Figure 2

Play blocks from found materials

Objective
To make some inexpensive large constructional blocks.

What you need
A large collection of same-sized, strong boxes such as washing powder packets (particularly those hard, almost-cubic ones with plastic handles), glue, gloss paint or vinyl wallpaper and paste.

What to do
Secure the lids down on the boxes with glue and, when thoroughly dry, either paint them with several coats of gloss paint (preferably in different colours) or cover them securely with wallpaper and paste. Let the children use them for building.

Variation
Other boxes, such as chocolate and shoe boxes, offer similar opportunities. Triangular chocolate boxes are interesting as they can be built into squares.

A take-apart table

Objectives
To allow children the opportunity to 'destruct' as well as construct, and to learn about the features of everyday objects.

What you need
Any old but safe household item such as a clock or piece of electrical equipment, cardboard, pens, magnifying lenses.

What to do
Lay out the lenses and the object attractively on a table. Add a notice saying 'Please find out about me'. Encourage the children to take the item apart, explore and examine each of the components, and discuss their properties, textures, shapes, forms, colours and feel.

Follow-up
When the item has been thoroughly explored the parts could be used to make a collage on card or material.

A 'home corner' with a difference

Objective
To provide stimulus areas to promote play and learning about different people, times, places, events, situations and so on.

What you need
A theme or focus related to your present topic, a planning meeting with adults and children, paper, pencils, paints, play equipment, coloured card.

What to do
Decide upon:
● the area of the classroom for the stimulus;
● your theme (a list of themes is provided on photocopiable page 85).

Discuss, preferably with the children, what the walls might look like and the furniture and costume requirements. Let the children design their own area, however simply.

When you have something with which everyone is satisfied, make up your stimulus area appropriately, adding signs, directions and posters.

Adults should also decide what additional 'learning' items they might provide: for example, would the area benefit from some books, writing or art equipment, a computer, calculators, cash register or money?

Instead of the usual 'Three can play here' sign, children could have tickets, passports, official badges, invitation cards or appointments.

Variations

• If the school has a spare classroom or wide corridor area, a stimulus area could be set up for the whole school which different groups can be timetabled to visit. If space permits, it may be possible to represent both a journey and a destination. If the past is represented you could have a time machine!

• Even a very small space, such as some shelving in the corner, can provide a tiny stimulus area for such things as a museum, art gallery, haberdashers, sock shop or tie and scarf shop.

I'm a computer!

Objectives
To help children understand how computers work and to have fun responding like a computer!

What you need
A very large, strong, cardboard box (packing from a fridge, for example), paints, glue, a craft knife, cardboard, scissors, 'mechanical' bits and pieces.

What to do
Paint and decorate the large box to represent a computer. Add a control panel and perhaps make a large keyboard with slots above each letter and number. Cogs, gears or lids can be stuck on for effect. Cut some slots at child height, big enough for cards to be pushed into and out of the computer. Next cut a door in one side, big enough for a child to go in and out and perhaps to put in a chair or two. Make some 'program' cards, some with questions, others with answers (see Figure 1).

Get a child to feed in a program card through the in-slot and another child to feed out the answer through the out-slot.

If alphabet cards are made for each letter, one child could feed in d–o–g and the other child could 'output' a picture of a dog.

Variation
The computer could be 'programmed' to read some poetry, using a tape-recorder, or sing a song, with the help of an individual child, from a card or button prompt.

Figure 1

Treasure hunt

Objective
To make the class base itself into an interesting and problem-solving experience.

What you need
A small toy.

What to do
Each day, select a different hiding place for the toy. Spend a few moments at the start of the session giving a few clues as to the hiding place. In the early days, let

a child find it easily but, as time goes on, let the hunt go on throughout the day, allowing the children to 'treasure hunt' in spare moments.

Variations
● Hide a different letter or number each day.
● Use arrows to take the children around the class base, getting them to look up, down and round.
● Give written or pictorial clues on card or sheets which the children can follow.

Quick and easy outdoor play

Objective
To increase the children's competence and mobility, control and co-ordination of developing muscles.

What you need
Playground chalk in different colours or playground paints for a more permanent feature.

What to do
Chalk out an 'adventure route' – perhaps related to a theme or topic – on the tarmac. Include the following:
● gaps to be jumped;
● zig-zag lines to be negotiated;
● spirals to be run around;
● stepping stones to be leapt onto;
● bean-bags to be thrown and caught;
● changing directions.
You could also add some symbols which mean children must stop and do things. They could be asked to jump three times each time they see the number '3', or to hop on one foot each time they see a rabbit.

Routes could be across a stream, through the jungle, skiing over mountains – any theme will do!

Children in wheelchairs can equally use these pathways provided they are made wide enough.

Variations
If space permits, an area of the classroom or cloakroom could similarly be set up for wet playtimes, using coloured tapes on the floor.

Come and play with us

Objective
To help parents understand the value of play and play materials in their children's development and learning.

What you need
Parents in the classroom, play materials, photocopiable page 86, pencils.

What to do
Ask the parents to play with a few children and a particular play material, for example, a constructional toy. While they are playing, suggest they try to identify on the prepared sheet on photocopiable page 86 anything they consider to be a part of 'learning' for the children.

Discuss with them at the end of the session their and your perceptions of the learning involved with this material.

Variations
• At a parents' evening show a video of children playing and ask the parents to 'analyse' the learning opportunities.
• Toy libraries can be extended by sending with each pack some questions or observation statements which parents can think about as they watch or involve themselves with the children's play.

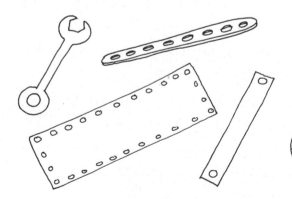

• Books of photographs of children playing with particular equipment can be compiled and sent home. Captions should offer information about what the children may be learning in each activity.

Adult involvement

Objective
For you to become an integral part of the children's play, and be able to assess learning opportunities.

What you need
Copies of photocopiable pages 87 and 88.

What to do
Negotiate a role for yourself in the children's play. For example, say 'I'd like to come and visit you in hospital today'. Make the role a realistic one – children do not expect adults suddenly to become bears or monsters – and you must take your lead from the children as to how much input you make.

Photocopiable pages 87 and 88 offer adults a means of assessing individual children's involvement and the potential for learning during these activities.

Follow-up
The adult, with sensitivity, can develop and extend children's views on cultural, racial and gender issues through sensitive and genuine intervention: 'I've bought Gurpreet some barfi or home-made chappatis' or 'I've got some flowers for Jason to make him feel better'.

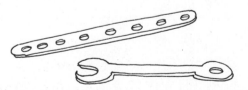

Planning and monitoring

Chapter six

Increasing moves towards greater accountability mean that early years practitioners are committing more information on teaching and learning to paper so that it can be shared with others and scrutinised to ensure it covers the curriculum and children's needs. Many early years teachers have welcomed this move (Campbell and Neill, 1992) and it has sharpened the focus on curriculum practices and planning for learning, as well as the need to monitor the quantity, quality and diversity of activities for individual children.

Planning and monitoring are the keystones for making high quality provision for learning. Each informs and extends the other in a cyclical process, from planning to monitoring and observing, to evaluating and assessing, to recording, to planning again.

In many establishments, greater openness and accountability has meant that practitioners have worked hard to involve parents and carers. There is a danger, however, that the children can become the people to whom education is somehow 'done' rather than them having a key part in it.

The children themselves can and should be part of the selection and evaluation processes. Sharing learning intentions with children, allowing them choices, ensuring equality of opportunity for both sexes and across all ability levels and cultural and ethnic groups all need careful monitoring and must be planned for effectively and efficiently. There is also a growing need for teachers and other professionals to acknowledge their own roles as learners in the classroom in order to be truly reflective practitioners.

The activities in this chapter are intended to heighten adults' awareness of daily teaching and learning interactions in the class base and to develop ideas about how effective and efficient these are and what the opportunities are for improvement.

Being clear about what you want

Objective
To ensure you and the children are clear about the learning intentions behind activities and events.

What you need
Copy of photocopiable page 89.

What to do
Discuss with children what they will do in a particular session and how they should do it. Follow this up by also telling children *why* they are doing that

particular activity: 'This should help you to think about . . .', 'I think you might learn a lot about . . .' or 'This will help you to understand about . . .'. If you are not always clear about this yourself, try writing some ideas down first. A sample planning sheet is given on photocopiable page 89.

Follow-up
You could tape-record yourself giving instructions so that you can judge their clarity for yourself!

What shall we do today?

Objective
To rethink the systematic planning of a varied and balanced set of activities for the children and the role of the adult in supporting and extending them.

What you need
Copies of photocopiable pages 90 and 91, a group meeting, a pen.

What to do
Having decided on the main areas of focus for activities in a particular week plot them on a planning sheet (photocopiable pages 90 or 91). Does this represent a balanced curriculum? Are

What to do

Draw up a chart like that shown in Figure 1 and photocopy it onto large A3 sheets. Encourage the children to look at the chart and decide what activity they would like to do with a friend.

Get the children to draw pictures of themselves and their partners in the centre of the chart, preferably holding hands. They should then map, each in a different coloured pen, where they are going to go. Lines could be numbered '1', '2', '3' and so on if the children are capable of selecting a series of activities rather than just one.

Variations

• The adult could select the children to work together by placing their names or photographs in the centre of the chart.
• The adult could draw themselves in the centre and ask which child would like to work with them at the painting table, in the finding-out area and so on, using the occasion for adult direction.

there sufficient opportunities for children to use physical skills and prowess? Will the activities be stimulating to *all* children? Are there particular activities which individuals should be guided towards? Make your plans accordingly.

Next consider which areas will need major adult support in order to extend the learning from the activity. Will individual children need support or extension? Who can provide this? Plot adult involvement (a colour key is usually the most appropriate) in order to ensure maximum learning opportunities.

Follow-up

The same kind of planning can be used to involve parent or student helpers.

Let's do it together

Objective

To allow children opportunities to plan to do activities together and share in experiences and results.

What you need

A3 sheets of paper, a photocopier, felt-tipped pens.

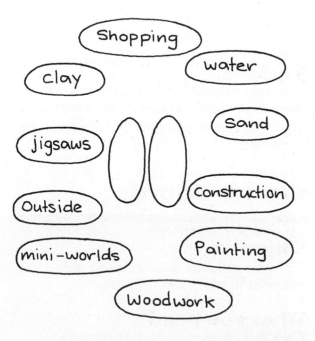

Figure 1

Didn't I do well!

Objectives
To help adults — and children — know what they have achieved that day or week and to encourage them to assess the activities.

What you need
Paper, pens, name labels.

What to do
If the children can write their own names you need a sheet drawn up with columns for names and three boxes to the right in which are drawn a smiley face, a sad face and a neutral face. If children cannot write their own names you need either sticky name labels or a list of their names which they can recognise and tick or colour.

Place a sheet by each activity. Train each child to 'sign out' by writing (or ticking) their names and ticking (or colouring in) an appropriate 'face':
- smiley for 'I've enjoyed that';
- sad for 'I didn't like that';
- neutral for 'I don't know'.

Variation
The sheets could be used as tick-lists to show that children have completed the activities. For older children they could be extended to include a written comment.

Choice boards

Objective
To allow children to select their own activities in a predetermined way.

What you need
Cork or polystyrene tiles, card, pens, string, mapping pins.

What to do
Make a 'choice board' from the tiles for each area of activity within the class base (see Figure 1). Label it, giving pictorial clues and words as relevant, and push in a number of mapping pins well spaced (you could use different colours for each activity area).

Make a name card with string attached for each child and hand them out. Ask the children to decide where they wish to work during the next session and get them to hang their name label over a mapping pin on the relevant choice board.

Variation
Photographs or children's drawings of themselves could be used instead of name cards. If children are used to selecting more than one activity they can number their name cards in sequence.

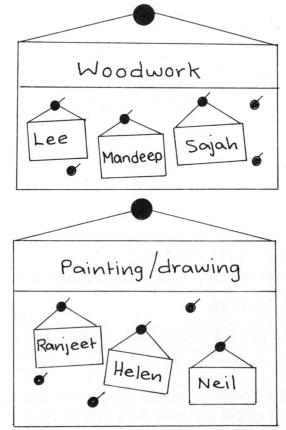

Figure 1

Making the most of diversity

Objectives
To consider provision in relation to children's ethnic and cultural backgrounds and to ensure all children feel their home circumstances are represented in the class base.

What you need
Your plans for presenting a new topic, a class list.

What to do
Scrutinise your class list and identify, if you haven't done so already, the range of backgrounds from which children come. Consider not only different ethnic groups but different cultural groups, the balance of sexes and age range.

Examine the plans you have made and see how far the features you have identified are represented. For example, if your topic is food, does the café area represent food from a range of different countries and cultures? Will topic books, pictures and posters show children from different cultural and ethnic backgrounds? Will the home corner or shop be attractive to both boys and girls?

Adjust your plans where you find any deficiencies. Teachers' centres, libraries, bookshops and publishers' representatives may all be able to help in finding more relevant materials. Parents from different ethnic and religious backgrounds are often extremely willing to loan items for the home corner or do a cooking session for you and the children.

NB It is also important to examine all materials to make sure people are represented in an unstereotypical way.

Questions, questions

Objective
To promote children's talk rather than adults'.

What you need
A tape-recorder.

What to do
Think about how you communicate with children. Perhaps tape-record a 'chat' session with children and listen to it later. When they bring something to show you, do you immediately start asking questions such as 'What colour is it?' 'What shape is it?' When you approach children engaged in a task, do you enter their activity with a question? Research has shown that questions act as weighty controls and deter children from genuinely communicating their thoughts and feelings (Wood and Wood, 1986; Tizard and Hughes, 1984; Wells, 1987).

It is vital to consider other ways of communicating which are less 'teacherly' and geared to eliciting more open responses from the children: 'Tell me about . . .', 'I bet mummy would be interested to see you . . .', 'That's an unusual way to . . .'. Communicate as a genuine talking partner rather than as a teacher.

Follow-up
When listening to recorded dialogues with children analyse the amount of conversation time each talking partner takes. Although we all want children to become linguistically competent, adults still tend to do the majority of the talking.

Constructive feedback

Objectives
For adults to question the genuineness of their response to children's activities and to encourage children to evaluate their work.

What you need
An activity and a child with whom you are interacting.

What to do
False praise is worthless and potentially damaging (Holt, 1991). When a child comes to show you a model or piece of finished work it is very easy to say 'That's lovely dear — go and put it over there'! Good feedback helps children to become constructively critical of their own efforts and achievements. Next time, ask:
- What do I really feel about this 'work'?
- Is it the best this child can do?
- What is the child's opinion of what has been achieved?
- Is everything 'lovely' or are there features of the work which might be improved?

NB If the 'product' is art work, adults

need to take care not to impose too many adult perceptions on a representation but should listen to what the child has to say about it.

Computer instructions

Objectives
To let the children see a computer as a teaching tool and to make the computer 'interactive'.

What you need
A computer with a word processing or drawing package, a printer, paper.

What to do
Instead of giving children verbal instructions about some writing, drawing or information-finding activity, use the computer to give the children, on screen, a series of questions or statements about what to do. You will have to program these in before the session begins. Let the children add their responses and print them out as a record. For example, a text might ask questions about the child: What is your name? How old are you? What is your favourite toy? A gap would be left after each question (or a box inserted) in which the child can give the answer.

For children who cannot yet read, the Concept Keyboard with a pictorial overlay is an equally effective way of developing this skill. Many teachers' centres have electronic scanners so that picture images can be imported onto the screen. In addition, children love to have an adult 'scribe' sitting with them at the computer and many parents feel the activity is an opportunity to contribute to their children's learning.

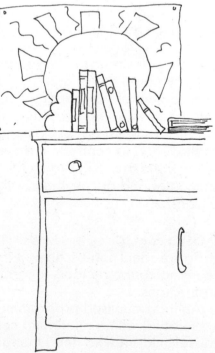

Learning centres

Objective
To offer an interesting, self-contained resource in the classroom where learning is focused on one particular aspect and children can work individually or in pairs, with or without an adult.

What you need
An idea for a learning centre (for example, 'Looking at Leaves'), relevant pictures and resources, posters, useful equipment such as magnifying lenses, Plasticine or dough, pencils, paper, scissors.

What to do
'Learning centres can take various forms but require an area of the classroom where children can go to look, touch, talk, play, write and problem-solve alone and together' (Briggs and Potter, 1990). Set up your learning centre so that it satisfies such requirements. You can include riddles and puzzles in pictures or words, things to explore, experiments to do, pictures to look at, books and anything else relevant to your focus.

Think about the design, shape, position and content of the learning centre and set one or more up accordingly.

Once established, explain the purpose of the learning centre to children and allow them to use it. Watch for learning outcomes and discuss them with the children.

Follow-up
• Pre-readers can be helped to use the learning centre by tape-recording instructions.
• An individualised programme can be developed within a learning centre for those children who need the facility.

Learning all the time

Objective
For children to be made aware that activities are designed to help them learn.

What you need
Time set aside following the completion of an activity or play session.

What to do
Seat the children around you and ask 'What did you learn while you were . . .?' As children are unfamiliar with being asked this type of question you may have to prompt them by referring back to your planned learning intentions. Try to be open in your responses, even though the children's answers may not be what you expected!

Speaking in turn

Objective
To monitor the equality of opportunity for girls and boys to speak in the class base.

What you need
A notebook, a pen and, if possible, an observer.

What to do
During an adult–children discussion, monitor how many times the adult speaks to boys and how many times to girls. Monitor, also, to which sex the adult directs questions or statements. Are they equally directed towards boys and girls?

Once you are aware of any differential in speaking opportunities given to the sexes, you can work towards greater equality for both.

Follow-up
A session could be tape-recorded and a tally made of speaking turns.

Carpet time

Objective
To monitor the effective use of the 'carpet area'.

What you need
A notebook, a pencil.

What to do
Note down all the times in the day when the carpet area is used and for how long. What percentage of the full day does this constitute? Does this lead you to believe that the carpet area could be better used? How?

Make any necessary changes to your plans to ensure the carpet area is used more effectively; for example, wheel the computer into the area, put reading or language games there, use puppets or create role-play opportunities.

Make sure that whatever you put in the carpet area is easy to move to allow for times when the carpet is needed for whole-class activities.

Recording who does what and when

Objective
To monitor children's activities during the day and week in order to ensure curriculum balance and progress.

What you need
Photocopiable page 92, a pencil.

What to do
Either as you generally observe the class or from the result of the children's own monitoring sheets, fill in the photocopiable page 92 according to what each child did.

From a straightforward 'quantity' statement with a tick, this could develop into a 'quality' statement by the addition of a quality key, for example, A, B, C or 1, 2, 3, where A or 1 is high quality understanding or performance and C or 3 is the poorest level.

Train them and trust them!

Objective
To ensure children safely use potentially dangerous equipment.

What you need
Potentially dangerous materials such as sharp scissors, woodwork tools.

What to do
Let the children in small groups handle the equipment, telling them of its dangerous features, for example, its sharpness, jagged edges and heaviness.

Talk about the need to keep ourselves safe and be responsible for our own welfare, giving examples such as crossing the road and learning to swim.

Next, show the children — and train them in — safe handling of the equipment. Show them how scissors should be carried with the points clutched firmly in the fist, that saws need a tooth-guard and so on.

Follow-up
Adults should identify all potentially dangerous materials and ensure that their children are systematically trained, at relevant times, to handle them safely.

Working as a team

Chapter seven

Many early years settings present practitioners with the extra challenge of working in a collaborative team. Even where teachers work alone, there are a number of adult helpers and parallel professionals whom they will encounter in the class base at various times. This is as it should be for we need to remember that children are not solitary learners but learn through interaction with others and the world around them (Wood, 1988).

Parents are indeed the child's first educators and, in early years settings, their role will be crucial in ensuring that home and school work are in harmony. Partnership between parents and teachers in early education must be a two-way process in which information is sought and gained on both sides. It is sometimes forgotten that children take their role models not only from adults but also from other children. Parallel and older peers can and do constitute ideal partners in the learning process.

Managerial and organisational tasks are essential in creating a smooth-running system in which all participants operate. It is, however, vital that such tasks are dealt with in the least time possible so that the maximum time can be spent on the children's learning.

There are several different kinds of communication and interaction which can ease the regular transition from home to the early years setting and back again, as well as ensure the learning environment is purposeful and effective. Teams of people working together have many decisions to make in relation to being consistent, distributing tasks equitably, planning and delegating tasks and responsibilities. These are explored in the activities that follow.

Meet the team!

Objectives
To introduce the staff of the base to visitors and, in the early days, to children and to act as a reminder of people's roles and responsibilities.

What you need
Large photographs of each member of staff showing them at work in their usual role, a staff notice board, card, pens.

What to do
Make and display a large sign, 'Hello from the staff of class . . .'. Mount the photographs on card and add a caption giving the name and a brief job description – this could be done in speech bubbles. Display these on the notice board (perhaps in alphabetical order) so that visitors are clear about who everyone is and are reminded of names and roles. This is particularly useful at the start of term but also needs a regular place when, for example, alternative carers escort children.

If jobs regularly rotate then these could be put on to separate caption cards and moved near to the responsible person.

Do not forget to include photographs of regular parent helpers and to add captions in different languages as appropriate.

Variation
Staff photographs could show them doing something they enjoy in their spare time. This introduces a 'human' element.

Planning together

Objective
To ensure all adults work collaboratively for the good of the children and do not overlap any more than necessary in their workloads.

What you need
A planning sheet.

What to do
When plans for children's learning tasks are complete, decide in a meeting who will be mainly responsible for what and ensure that each of you is clear about this, and so are the children. A notice posted each day keeps parents and carers informed and makes it possible for class base visitors to locate the appropriate person.

Involving other adults

Objective
To ensure classroom helpers feel important and wanted and are clear about their responsibilities.

What you need
Paper, a pen.

What to do
Having planned clearly what you want the children to do and learn, pass the information on either in writing or verbally to the helper. It is useful to give

them some notes about what to look for, especially if they are relatively new to the situation.

Knowing what learning is intended and what it is useful to look for empowers the helper to take a high level of responsibility for the task.

Follow-up
It may be appropriate to ask helpers for a brief written note of achievements if there is unlikely to be time to talk at the end of the session.

Who cleans the paint pots?

Objective
To examine the distribution of tasks to different personnel and agree on the best arrangement for a smooth-running class base.

What you need
A decision-making meeting, job descriptions for all personnel if available, a pen, paper.

What to do
Draw up a list of the mundane but necessary jobs which must be done daily and weekly, such as cleaning paint pots, filling water trays, cleaning out sand trays, keeping the clay in good condition and so on.

Discuss openly and honestly how these jobs can best be accomplished and by whom. It may be that you decide a rotation system is the most viable or that certain job descriptions require specific work to be done by individuals.

Follow-up
Writing the jobs down on a chart or rota saves any potential arguments later!

You are here

Objective
To help visitors, new parents and children find their way to your class base and around the school generally.

What you need
A large ground plan of the school, pens, brightly coloured card, glue.

What to do
Display the plan of the school (in its correct orientation). Make a brightly coloured arrow or pointing finger. Stick it onto the plan to indicate where people are standing as they look at the map. Make a label saying 'You are here' to add alongside. Perhaps also label the reception office, headteacher's office and other major features of the school.

Dealing with interruptions

Objective
To keep unnecessary interruptions from children and adults to a minimum.

What you need
Cardboard, a pen, string or Blu-Tack.

What to do
To keep interruptions from children to a minimum:
• make sure that children know what to do if they are stuck or want to show you something (they could put their hands up, go to a certain adult for help or show each other);
• do not allow yourself to be interrupted when you have clearly said it is not appropriate – be firm!
    To keep adult interruptions to a

minimum during, for example, story time or discussion time, make a cheerful but firm notice to hang on the class door saying 'Please do not interrupt us now' or 'Please come back in ten minutes' with an appropriate picture.

Follow-up
It is useful to raise the question of interruptions at a main staff meeting. It is quite usual to find that everyone is sick of the same regular interruptions, and decisions can be made to reduce them.

Setting learning goals

Objectives
To become more specific when setting goals for children's learning, and to ensure adults can watch for learning and the children can show achievement.

What you need
A meeting in which to share ideas about individual children, notes about specific goals and learning objectives.

What to do
When adults set objectives for children they are usually intending that something will be learned! For this to happen effectively, it is necessary to distinguish between vague objectives and those which are more specific. Otherwise, it may not be clear to you what you really want the children to achieve, in which case, it certainly will not be clear to them!
    As an example, 'Peter should learn to jump better' or 'Rajinder should learn to build a house' are vague, whereas specific goals would be:
• 'Peter should be able to jump 10/15/20 times without stopping';
• 'Rajinder should be able to build a

model of a house three storeys high with six windows and two doors'.

Specific goals mean that adults and children have the joy of registering an achievement and there is a genuine opportunity for praise and further goal setting. With vague goals, no one knows whether an achievement has really occurred or not.

That special day

Objective
To create a special day for a specific purpose, geared also to generating the interest of children, parents and the whole early years team.

What you need
A focus, such as teddy bears.

What to do
Plan to have a special focus day, for example, children could all bring in their teddy bears or other cuddly toys (it could also be pets, favourite story-books, favourite toys, baby photographs). Set a date and inform parents in writing or verbally well in advance.

Arrange the classroom to create space and, on the day, offer the children a range of learning opportunities: teddies can be weighed, measured, classified according to height, texture, colour; they can be written about, photographed, painted and drawn; or have a picnic prepared by the children.

Any activity which ensures children realise that learning is all around them would be suitable. At the end of the day, there might be a 'teddy assembly' or 'teddy tea' to which parents and school staff are invited.

Make me a story

Objectives
To encourage peer collaboration across the school and to give children a purpose for talking and reading.

What you need
Matched pairings of older children from within the school with your children, pens, paper.

What to do
Organise some class times when the pairs of children can meet. When a pair is together encourage the older child to write a story for the young child by first discussing together what types of story, characters, illustrations, length and so on, the younger child enjoys. The older child will actually be conducting an interview and making notes. It may be necessary to have several chats with opportunities for the older child to draft and redraft the writing as necessary.

The final book should be illustrated and given a proper cover with the author's name and copyright marking. This gives the younger children a library of purpose-made story-books — and the older children great esteem!

Follow-up
Older children could help younger children by devising simple maths or science games by first finding out what the younger children like and what game would be appropriate to their level and interests.

Yes, I mean it!

Objective
To ensure consistency and fairness in dealing with children.

What you need
An observer, a pen, paper.

What to do
Think about how often you and other members of the team *say* you will do something but don't. For example, you might say 'I won't listen to you unless you put your hand up' and then promptly respond to a child shouting out! Try to monitor if and when you do this kind of thing; get another adult to observe and make notes for you if possible.

Once you know how often and when you do this, it is usually easy to become more consistent.

This week's focus is . . .

Objective
To share with parents, other adults and visitors what the children in your class will be thinking about over the next week or two.

What you need
A notice board, cardboard, felt-tipped pens, planning sheets.

What to do
Clear your notice board and place it near the entrance to the class base. Label it appropriately: 'This week we are thinking about . . .' or 'Our topic this week is . . .'. Add your planning sheet and some related pictures, paintings, drawings or models produced by the children. You might add a notice: 'Do you have anything you could share with us about our topic?' or 'Topic pictures, books and artefacts will be welcomed!'

Variation
If no wall space is available a topic newsletter might be produced with similar contents, using a single A3 folded page, and distributed to relevant adults.

What are we doing today?

Objective
To keep parents and carers informed of things it would be useful for children to talk about at home.

What you need
A small notice board, timetables, a pen, paper.

What to do
Place the notice board near the entrance to the class base. Each day, post a timetable of the day's main activities to be undertaken by the children and adults. A brief note of why certain things are to be done is informative. For example, 'Cooking soup helps us with our maths and science and we love to eat it!' Surround the notice with children's drawings and paintings or photographs of the activities.

Variation
A single-page newsletter for parents about the new topic each time it changes frequently prompts parents to arrange appropriate visits or buy related books.

'Our topic this week is Our Pets'

Sharing what we do

Objective
To help parents, carers and other adults understand the learning and enjoyment behind different learning situations.

What you need
Photograph albums, photographs of classroom events, a word-processor, paper.

What to do
Either as a class team of adults (or preferably with the children) sort the photographs into various categories so that they can be given labels, such as 'we like to cook' or 'we like to play in the shop'. For each category, put the photographs in a suitable sequence so you can explain in writing what is happening and what the children are likely to be learning. Write or word-process captions for each picture and mount the whole into an album.

Save some photographs for the front cover and make a montage, adding a suitable title.

Several books can be made, kept in the nursery and read as 'stories' by the children or, better still, children and parents can take them home on a library system.

I love you really!

Objective
To ensure that a misbehaving child retains good feelings about him or herself.

What you need
No special requirements.

What to do
Discuss with the child the problem regarding their inappropriate behaviour. Make sure the behaviour comes in for 'blame' and not the child. For example, do not say 'Sarah, you really are a naughty girl!' but instead, 'Sarah, that was really not very nice to throw sand at Jasbir — none of us like that kind of behaviour.' If the child herself is directly blamed this can severely damage her self-esteem and usually only leads to poorer behaviour.

Follow-up
Adults should never be afraid to point out to a child that their behaviour is causing them distress or hurt. Young children normally want to please adults.

Listen very carefully

Objectives
To ensure instructions are given to children clearly and only once in order to save time, and to check your instructions to children are clear and unambiguous.

What you need
A tape-recorder.

What to do
Ensure that when you or other adults give an instruction to children you stop them, explain clearly — and only once — what they have to do and then set them about the task. Listen to each other and note if the same instructions are given more than once. If they are, resolve to do better next time!

Alternatively, record yourself giving children instructions and information.

Listen to the recording and try to follow what your said step by step. How clear were your instructions? Did they fit your intentions? Did your words and manner make it possible for the children to set about their activities?

Follow-up
If you tape-recorded the session try to get someone who was not there to listen to the tape and attempt to think through or follow your instructions, giving feedback on clarity, sequence and repetition.

Supply personnel welcome!

Objective
To make supply teachers (and others) feel welcome, needed and part of the school and class base.

What you need
Information sheets about the school and class base, copies of current planning sheets, daily outline timetable, a class list, a folder, preferably a photograph of the class, cardboard, crayons, perhaps a note of welcome from the headteacher.

What to do
Put together a pack of useful materials about the school and the class, including a photograph of the class if this is available. (It is useful if you can write the names of children directly onto the photograph.) Get the children to make a 'welcome' card and include this.

When you know in advance that a supply teacher or student is coming, send the pack by post so that the person gets a feel for the school and class before they arrive.

Using helpers' strengths

Objective
To ensure that adult helpers are clear about their role and are used to the best of their abilities.

What you need
Paper, a typewriter or word-processor, copy of photocopiable page 93.

What to do
There are likely to be a range of people who are willing to help in the class base; as well as parents, there may be grandparents and other extended family members.

Having identified people who would like to help, ensure that they are sent and complete (either with you or on their own) an information sheet about their strengths and interests. A sample sheet is given on photocopiable page 93. If helpers are from other ethnic groups, it would be helpful either to go through the sheet orally with them or ensure that the letter they receive is in their own language. Make sure your helpers are then given corresponding tasks.

Variation/Follow-up
Do check with helpers periodically whether any of the original information has changed.

Getting to know others

Objectives
For practitioners to extend their own understanding of different styles of class management and organisation, and to make contact with kindred spirits!

What you need
A camera, a notebook, a pen.

What to do
Make arrangements for one member of the team to visit another setting, with both a general and a specific idea of what to look at. It could be any setting but should, where possible, include aspects dissimilar to your own, for example, nurseries run by different organisations as well as other education authorities, playgroups and crèches.

While there, observe, take notes, discuss and take photographs. Make some general and specific notes on both the setting and the predetermined organisational and management issues to share with colleagues in your own setting.

Organise a meeting to share your thoughts and ideas. If possible, include staff from both the settings.

Variations
● It is useful for one or more team members to make a visit together as it gives the benefit of shared perceptions.
● Visits can be extended to offering each other ideas, equipment and other resources (including human resources).

Time to observe and reflect

Chapter eight

Observation is rarely wasted time but adults always seem to suffer pangs of guilt if they take time to stand back and watch! We often need to convince ourselves that observation is a vital and commendable adult activity in the class base and that adults and children will benefit from it.

Teaching young children requires the ongoing interpretation of classroom events and interactions, which means we are constantly thinking on our feet. This leads to immediate reactions. Often, there is no time to think through what is happening and to be proactive rather than reactive (Pollard and Tann, 1987). There needs to be a balance established between reacting swiftly and making general ongoing decisions, and standing back to think more clearly about classroom events.

If time is wasted because children are taking too long to settle in their tasks, or because children misbehave, it is all too easy to blame them without recognising that some of the difficulties may be of our own making, and are within our own control to change. We can and must do so by taking the time to analyse and evaluate our practices.

In relation to the never-ending problem of time, unfortunately one often has to use time to find out how to save it! This chapter seeks to help practitioners explore time management and to encourage teachers to think through their own practices.

Being a wise owl

Objective
To create time and personal space in order to observe classroom activities.

What you need
A large owl (or similar creature) made out of felt or cardboard which is big enough to be seen from across the classroom but which can be pinned onto the adult's shoulder.

What to do
Tell the children a story about a 'wise owl' who carefully watched what was happening all around her and could always help people. Tell them that sometimes you are going to be a wise owl and that, instead of talking to the children, you are going to watch them carefully. When they see the owl on your shoulder, they are under no circumstances to talk to you otherwise you will not be able to watch so well. Do not forget to tell them what to do when they are 'stuck', such as help each other or go to another adult.

Make sure that the observation is no longer than 10 to 20 minutes depending upon the age and maturity of the children.

Monitoring adult activities

Objective
For adults to make the best possible use of class time for interacting with children.

What you need
A time-grid (photocopiable page 94), a pencil.

What to do
Sample your time at any given period in the day to find out what you are doing. Take a half-hour period at different times on different days and mark on the time-grid on photocopiable page 94 what you are doing each minute.

Add up these periods of time and see how much time you spend doing what. You may well get a surprise! If too much time is spent on organisation and management, you will need to think, and perhaps talk to colleagues, about how more of this time might be spent with the children.

Variations

• Each member of the team could undertake this activity for another.
• The time-scale could be as short as 20-second sampling if you want to be precise about your time use.
• It is possible to do the same kind of thing for individual children, particularly those about whom you are concerned or who appear to do very little in a day.

Did I speak to you?

Objective

To find out how many times in a particular day or week you interact with individual children and for how long.

What you need

Paper, a pencil.

What to do

Determine that today you will note down each time you speak to individual children. Devise a simple record of recording, as in Figure 1. Mark each interaction, as shown.

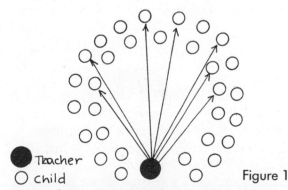

● Teacher
○ Child

Figure 1

At the end of the day write down the names of the children you have:
• not spoken to at all;
• spoken to only fleetingly;
• spoken to in more than one sentence;
• spoken to in an interactive way (a conversation).

Do the same for a few days. Are there children with whom you interact more than others? Are there children with whom you rarely have interactions? Armed with this information it is possible to redress the balance by conscious effort!

Variation

You could target a few children each day over a period of a week and see how much interaction you have with those children, building up to a picture of all the children in a few weeks.

Getting it taped

Objective

To free adults so they can work with groups and individuals.

What you need

Audio-tape and a recorder, relevant play material, a notebook, a pen.

What to do

Make a tape for the children so they can play independently. The following example uses a farm layout and animals.

First, briefly play with the farm layout, animals, tractors and buildings yourself to discover their potential. Depending on the age of the children, prepare some instructions which might go with the farm: 'There are three cows in the big field. Turn off the tape while you put the cows in the big field. The tractor is ploughing the little field and three people are working there. Can you put the tractor and the workers in the little field? Turn off the tape while you do.' When children get familiar with the farm they can be asked to make a farm building with bricks. This allows both children and adults a period of independence.

Try out the tape yourself with the children first so that you can make any necessary adjustments. You must remember to tell the children when to turn the tape off, if not in words then with a recorded signal like a small bell.

It is useful to have a basic diagram or picture of what the finished farm layout should look like as a learning check.

Time's nearly up!

Objective
To allow the children opportunities to think about time running out.

What you need
No special requirements.

What to do
Ensure that about five minutes from the end of the session children have some kind of warning that they need to complete their task or bring it to a point where they can happily leave it. It could be a verbal signal or a clock alarm could be set off. Everyone could be told at once or adults could circulate, informing groups. It could also be a time when children are allocated a space to store or display the results of their activities.

Seeing what you think

Objective
To enable adults to be clear about the differences between observation and interpretation.

What you need
A notebook, a pencil.

What to do
Choose a particular child to observe for a ten-minute period. Jot down what you actually see happening as far as you can. When convenient read your notes, preferably with someone else. Have you been really objective or put in additional subjective information?

Compare these two statements:
• Sam using a bucket and spade in the sand with Surekha and Amrit; filling and emptying the bucket for a full 10-minute period. There was no verbal interaction between the children but Surekha watched Sam on three occasions and then attempted to emulate Sam's actions.
• Sam was having a wonderful time playing with the sand tray; he really enjoyed playing with Surekha and Amrit and they all seemed to get a lot out of it. They didn't communicate but just enjoyed playing alongside each other and doing things together.

The differences may be subtle but they are extremely important. In the first we have the facts of the situation. In the second we have an interpretation which may or may not be accurate.

Sandpit

Moving around easily

Objective
To consider the movement of human traffic during the day and any existing or potential 'jams' which are unnecessary and time-wasting.

What you need
A little time for you (or a colleague) to observe the movement of adults and children around the room.

What to do
Ask yourself the following:
● Where have I got stuck today trying to move around the base?
● Where have I seen children pushing each other to get by?
● Where have I had to wait for other adults or children, or climb over resources?
● Have any areas created particular problems for children or adults with special needs?

  Observe each area. If there is too much furniture rearrange it. Find out if there is any you can really do without or move elsewhere. Are there too many children in that area? Why? Check whether the other activities are sufficiently interesting or attractive. Are there too many adults in the area? Why? See whether staff are clear about their timetable of activities. Is the area located too near a door or opening? Ask the children and other staff for their thoughts, too. Rearrange the layout as necessary.

Keeping materials in good order

Objective
To ensure that materials always look attractive to use and are clean and safe for children without taking any adult time.

What you need
Warm and clean soapy water, small brushes, cloths, a water tray, a hair-dryer.

What to do
Periodically have a wash day with a difference! Instead of general play with the (washable) materials, get the children cleaning and drying them. This is a good scientific activity and will also allow sorting opportunities.

Tidy-up time

Objectives
To make tidy-up time easier for the children and to save your time.

What you need
No special requirements.

What to do
There are at least three things you can do to create valuable time at this juncture:
• Stop all the children and get them to sit in the carpet area. From there, allocate jobs to individuals, a few at a time, while the rest of the children read counting rhymes, say poems or sing songs.
• Stop all the children and ask them to stand perfectly still. Get them to look around the classroom and list some of the things which need to be put away. Again, allocate tasks to certain children or pairs of children, or have a 'helper list' so that everyone takes turns on different weeks.
• As before, stop the children. Next identify certain areas in which materials should be placed (paint pots on the sink, glue pots on the cupboard top, and so on) and nominate children to take them there while the rest put other materials in the centre of the table or floor space. In turn, they can then return their materials to the appropriate place without every child being on the move at the same time.

The teacher should stand still throughout and offer positive praise to those children who are putting things away in the prescribed manner.

NB Always make sure that at some time in the week all children are responsible for tidying up after themselves and others.

Follow-up
Let the children have the right sized tools for cleaning. For example, shorten the handles on brooms or mops.

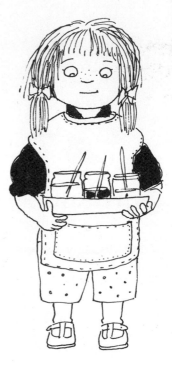

Have we got time?

Objective
For children to begin to understand time limits and make plans for effective time use.

What you need
A timer.

What to do
When time for a task is limited, tell the children, 'We have only five minutes before you go home. Shall we sing some songs or have a story?' Ask the children why they make particular choices and help them to estimate the time it takes to do something.

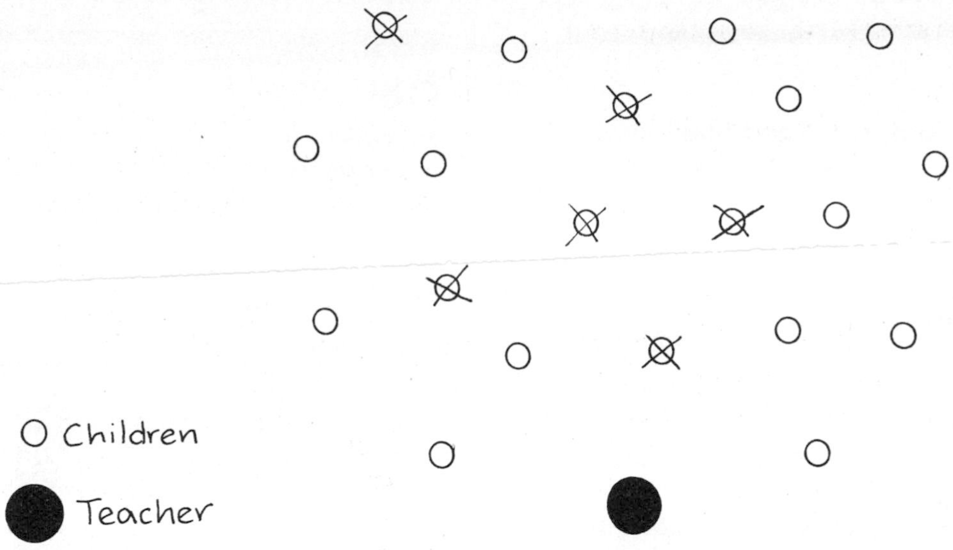

O Children

● Teacher

Figure 1

Gather round

Objective
To see where and upon which children the adult focus mainly rests during circle-time discussions.

What you need
A notebook, a pen.

What to do
Draw a plan of the children's seating arrangement and each time your eye or voice comes to rest on a particular child tick or cross that position in the circle as in Figure 1. Did you make contact with all the children or mostly the ones in the centre of vision? Were there any particular areas which had little or no contact? Make a conscious effort to look in other directions.

Follow-up
Either change the seating arrangement so all the children are in the central field of vision or ensure that, during the next circle-time, you scan the edges of the group as well as the middle.

Evaluating your organisation

Objective
To note times and places when organisation does not run smoothly and to take remediating action.

What you need
A notebook, a pencil.

What to do
Note down each time an element of the organisation of the class base does not run smoothly and, if you can, note why. Get other adults to do this as well. Share these notes between you and make a composite list. Next take one event from the list at a time and examine the effect of each (how it makes you and the children feel), then try to identify its causes and whether it is recurrent.

What solutions are available to you? Perhaps clearer instructions need to be given to the children, perhaps the adults are not clear about their responsibilities, or perhaps materials need relocating.

Priority listings

Objective
To make decisions about priorities.

What you need
A notebook, a pen.

What to do
Make a list of the things you want to do that day. Examine your list and prioritise them according to those things which you must do first, those you feel you should do and those you would like to do if time allows (Arnold, 1991). Follow the list and do the activities in their set order.

Follow-up
Anything left on the list needs re-examining before it is placed on the next day's list. Anything which keeps getting shunted around may not actually be necessary anyway!

Time for you!

Objective
To ensure that the 'whole' person within every early years practitioner has time to develop and be catered for!

What you need
No special requirements.

What to do
It is very simple! Decide that occasionally you must be yourself and do your own thing! We all have different tolerances to workloads but continuous work is not good for anyone. Force yourself to have two or more hours every week — or even day — when it is your time. So, take the telephone off the hook, leave the record books at school, forget your planning file and relax!
   Remember:
• that the class base and the school will be there long after you are;
• what does not get done today is either not worth doing or becomes tomorrow's priority.
• to congratulate yourself as often as possible on what you have achieved rather than constantly worrying about the things you have not done.

Balancing the day, see page 20

Planning sheet – week beginning

Activity	MONDAY	TUESDAY	WEDNESDAY	THURSDAY	FRIDAY
Cooking					
Construction (large)					
Construction (small)					
Talking: puppets, take-apart table, etc.					
Mini-worlds: farm, Playpeople, dolls house, etc.					
Mathematics					
Other					
Outside visits/walks					

Balancing the day, see page 20

Planning in seven areas of experience

Areas of experience	Focus of interest =
Linguistic and literary	
Human and social	
Scientific and technological	
Creative/ aesthetic	
Physical	
Mathematical	
Moral and spiritual	

A home corner with a difference, see page 51

A FEW IDEAS FOR STIMULUS AREAS

Generally, stimulus areas can be split into two main sections:
- imaginative/fantasy;
- pretend/sociodramatic.

In turn these can be broken down yet further into stimulus areas based on:
- stories;
- poetry/rhyme;
- imaginary 'worlds' (beyond child's experience); e.g. outer space, under-the-sea
- shops; e.g. greengrocers, chemist, jewellers
- services; e.g. post office, estate agent, museum, café
- 'invisible' commerce/industry; e.g. newspaper office

Several, of course, could be combined for we might have an imaginary world in which there are imaginary shops or a service in which something fantastic happens like being transported off into space from the travel agent — children's minds are much more fertile in terms of imagination than ours!
   The following ideas are particularly good for both cross-curricular links and sheer enjoyment!

Stories: Goldilocks and the Three Bears, Snow White and the Seven Dwarfs, Cinderella, The Enormous Pancake (Chappati), The Gingerbread Man, Christmas Story, Diwali Story, Lighthouse Keeper's Lunch, Jim and the Beanstalk — the possibilities are endless!

Rhymes/poetry: any which tell a story.

Imaginary worlds: under-the-sea, in space, pirate ship, jungle, haunted castle, dinosaur world, monster caves, snow den, animal homes, palace, castle.

Shops: grocers, greengrocers, chemist, jewellers, shoe shop, haberdashers, sock shop, tie shop, milliners, pet shop, joke shop, toy shops, pawn shop, handbag and cases shop, bookshop, clothes shop, garden shop, ironmongers, records/tapes/compact discs, fishmongers, milk and snack shop (for real!), perfumery, bakery, seaside shop.

Services: post office, bank, travel agent, theatrical costumier/dress hire, café, take-away, fish and chip shop, museum, clinic, casualty, dentists, estate agent, booking office ships/planes/trains/coaches, for sweetshop, nursery (either plants or babies!), citizens' advice bureau, repairers, builders, painter/decorators (especially outside!), bakery, weather station.

'Invisible' workplaces: newspaper office, pottery, production line, recording studio, television/radio studio, artist's studio, author's office, bookbinders, wallpaper manufacturer, printers.

Come and play with us, see page 54

PLAY ACTIVITY:	WHAT DID THE CHILDREN DO . . . ?
Wet sand with scoops and containers of different shapes and sizes	WHAT DID THE CHILDREN LEARN . . . ?

The children will probably want to:
- explore the sand, scoops and containers for a few minutes;
- make different sized sandcastles with the containers;
- discuss what they are doing in relation to what other children and the adult are doing.

The children will have the opportunity to learn:
- bigger containers hold more sand;
- small containers hold less sand;
- scoops are good for lifting fairly large amounts of sand;
- certain containers make better shapes for sandcastles;
- how wet/dry the sand is will make a better or worse sandcastle.

The children will begin to use words like:
- full;
- empty;
- containers/pots/tubs/buckets;
- holds more/most;
- holds less/least;
- holds the same.

As play develops, the children might like to have some:
- wide, flat containers;
- tall thin containers.

Adult involvement, see page 54

EVALUATION OF PLAY MATERIALS

Take the opportunity to play with a toy of some kind
(NB not everything will apply to every play resource)

The play material/equipment:

What is it made of?

What is it like to handle/experience?

What might be its purpose? State possible objectives/potential regarding children's development or learning, including influence on, in all or some of the following:

Social:
communication (verbal/non-verbal)
sharing and turn-taking
co-operation
role play
friendship

Intellectual:
concept formation
creative ideas
reasoning/logic
exploration/investigation
decision-making/problem-solving
facts/knowledge
colour and texture

Physical/manipulative/psychomotor:
fine/gross
spatial awareness
shape and form

Emotional/moral:
personal response likely from a child
control of emotions
sensitivity
self-concept, self-expression
enjoyment
care and respect for materials

Attitude/motivational qualities

How far is play with this equipment likely to present 'cognitive challenge'?

To what age range of children?

Difficulties in use/storage?

If you get a chance to play with this equipment with children, are their perceptions the same as yours?

Adult involvement, see page 54

INDIVIDUAL PLAY RECORD

Child's engagement in different forms of play	Some times	Rarely	Never	Comments
Solitary play				
Parallel play				
Co-operative play				
Role/fantasy play				
Mini-worlds play				
Constructional play				
Creative play with different materials				
Does the child . . .?				
Persist in the play and complete it to a satisfactory end?				
Engage in longer play sequences (2 minutes or more)?				
Develop progressively more complex play sequences?				
Invent new games or new activities?				
Disrupt other children's play?				
Have difficulty in choosing a play activity?				
Have difficulty in settling down to a play activity?				
Revert to lower levels of play than capable of?				
Show constant repetition of the same play?				
Other items				
Listens co-operatively and responds at carpet time				
Relates successfully to adults				
Communicates successfully				

Being clear about what you want, see page 56

ACTIVITIES	WHAT?	WHY?	WHO?
1. Themes – displays and 'specials'			
2. Creative/aesthetic drawing painting cutting modelling			
3. Natural materials, water tactile/environment clay sand seeds/pasta			
4. Science and technology			
5. Construction small large			
6. Domestic play home shop			
7. Mathematical experiences			
8. Physical play outdoor dance gymnastics			
9. Table activities			
10. Games			
11. Music, songs			
12. Stories, poems, rhymes			
13. Cooking			
14. Drink/snack time			

What shall we do today? see page 56

Planning sheet – week beginning

Activity	MONDAY	TUESDAY	WEDNESDAY	THURSDAY	FRIDAY
Water					
Sand					
Investigation (e.g. clay, spaghetti)					
Role play/ stimulus area					
Painting/ art					
Music/ sound					
Hand/eye co-ordination					
Gross physical	Outdoor play				

What shall we do today, see page 56

	9.00	9.30	9.50	10.30	11.30	1.30	2.00	3.00
MONDAY		Register Carpet time					Register Carpet time	PARENT ASSEMBLY
TUESDAY		Register Carpet time		HALL TIME			Register Carpet time	
WEDS		Register Carpet time	SCHOOL ASSEMBLY 10.10				Register Carpet time	HALL TIME
THURS		Register Carpet time					Register Carpet time	
FRIDAY		Register Carpet time	HALL TIME				Register Carpet time	

Recording who does what and when, see page 64

ACTIVITY MONITORING SHEET

Children's names / Achievement / Morning children						Comments
Afternoon children						

Using helpers' strengths, see page 74

Dear

I am so glad that you have expressed an interest in helping with activities in the classroom.

So that we can get an idea for the types of things you might like doing, it would be really helpful if you could tick anything on the following lists which you would be interested in – please add anything else we haven't thought of!

I really like:
    reading
    cooking
    sewing
    gardening
    writing
    drawing
    making things
    playing a musical instrument
    sports

Is there anything really special that you are very good at? We know there is lots of talent out there!

I would like to help children with:
    play activities
    art activities
    cooking
    reading
    writing
    making things
    mathematical activities
    science activities
    talking about experiences
    clay

We are really looking forward to working with you and hope to see you very soon.

Yours sincerely,

Monitoring adult activities, see page 76

Time / Activity	Time minute interval	Time minute interval	Time minute interval	Time minute interval	Time minute interval
With children					
Observing					
Talking with adults					
Organising materials etc.					
Administrative tasks					

Book list

Reference books

Arnold, R. (1991) 'Making the best use of teacher time'. In Craig, I. (Ed) *Managing the Primary Classroom*, Longman.

Athey, C. (1990) *Extending Thought in Young Children*, Paul Chapman.

Brierley, J. (1992) *Growth in Children*, Cassell.

Briggs, F. and Potter, G. (1990) *Teaching Children in the First Three Years of School*, Longman Cheshire.

Bruce, T. (1987) *Early Childhood Education*, Hodder and Stoughton.

Bruce, T. (1991) *Time to Play in Early Childhood*, Hodder and Stoughton.

Campbell, R. and Neill, S. (1992) *Teacher Time and Curriculum Manageability at Key Stage 1*, AMMA.

Craig, I. (Ed) (1991) (2nd Edn) *Managing the Primary Classroom*, Longman.

Cullingford, C. (1991) *The Inner World of the School: Children's Ideas About Schools*, Cassell.

Dunne, E. and Bennett, N. (1990) *Talking and Learning in Groups*, Macmillan.

Edwards, D. and Mercer, N. (1987) *Common Knowledge: The Development of Understanding in the Classroom*, Methuen.

Field, T. M. (1980) 'Pre-school play: Effects of teacher/child ratios and organisation of the classroom space', *Child Study Journal*, 10(3), 191–205.

Fisher, R. (1990) *Teaching Children to Think*, Blackwell.

Garvey, C. (1991) (2nd Ed) *Play*, Fontana.

Gentle, K. (1993) *Teaching Painting in the Primary School*, Cassell.

Grieve, R. and Hughes, M. (Eds) (1990) *Understanding Children: Essays in Honour of Margaret Donaldson*. Blackwell.

Hall, N. and Abbott, L. (1991) *Play in the National Curriculum*, Hodder and Stoughton.

Holt, J. (1991) *Learning All the Time*, Education Now.

Hutt, S. J., Tyler, S., Hutt, C. and Christopherson, H. (1989) *Play, Exploration and Learning: A Natural History of the Pre-School*, Routledge.

Jackson, M. (1987) 'Making sense of school'. In Pollard, A. (Ed) *Children and their Primary Schools*, Falmer Press.

Jones, V. F. and Jones, L. S. (1986) (2nd Edn) *Comprehensive Classroom Management: Creating Positive Learning Environments*, Allyn and Bacon Inc.

Kirklees Metropolitan Council (1985) *Guidelines for the Curriculum in the Early Years: A Discussion Document*, Kirklees L.E.A. (see Appendix on classifying and categorizing play materials).

McLean, S. V. (1991) *The Human Encounter: Teachers and Children Living Together in Pre-School*, Falmer Press.

Moyles, J. R. (1989) *Just Playing? The Role and Status of Play in Early Childhood Education*, Open University Press.

Moyles, J. R. (1991) *Play as a Learning Process in Your Classroom*, Mary Glasgow.

Moyles, J. R. (1992) *Organizing for Learning in the Primary Classroom: A Balanced Approach to Classroom Management*, Open University Press.

Moyles, J. R. (1993) 'Just a matter of routine . . .? Organising for learning in the early years classroom', *Education 3-13*, 21(1).

Nash, B. C. (1981) 'The effects of classroom spatial organisation on four and five year old children learning', *British Journal of Educational Psychology*, 51, 44–55.

Neill, S. R. St. J. (1991) *Classroom Non-Verbal Communication*, Routledge.

Pollard, A. and Tann, S. (1987) *Reflective Teaching in the Primary School: A Handbook for the Classroom*, Cassell.

Shipman, M. (1985) *The Management of Learning in the Classroom*, Hodder and Stoughton.

Smilansky, S. and Shefataya, S. (1990) *Facilitating Play: A Medium for Promoting Cognitive, Socio-Emotional and Academic Development in Young Children*, Psychosocial and Educational Publications.

Tizard, B. and Hughes, M. (1984) *Young Children Learning*, Fontana.

Wells, G. (1987) *The Meaning Makers: Children Learning Language and Using Language to Learn*, Hodder and Stoughton.

Wood, D. (1988) *How Children Think and Learn*, Basil Blackwell.

Wood, P. and Wood, H. (1986) 'Questioning the pre-school child', *Educational Review*, 35(2), 149–162.

Children's books

Hutchins, P. (1973) *Goodnight Owl*, Penguin Books.

Willis, J. (1981) *The Tale of Georgie Grub*, Anderson.

Ziefert, H. (1986) *Nicky's Noisy Night*, Penguin Books.